UNDERSTANDING
T. C. BOYLE

Understanding Contemporary American Literature
Matthew J. Bruccoli, Series Editor

Volumes on

Edward Albee • Sherman Alexie • Nicholson Baker • John Barth
Donald Barthelme • The Beats • The Black Mountain Poets
Robert Bly • T. C. Boyle • Raymond Carver • Fred Chappell
Chicano Literature • Contemporary American Drama
Contemporary American Horror Fiction
Contemporary American Literary Theory
Contemporary American Science Fiction, 1926–1970
Contemporary American Science Fiction, 1970–2000
Contemporary Chicana Literature • Robert Coover • James Dickey
E. L. Doctorow • Rita Dove • John Gardner • George Garrett
John Hawkes • Joseph Heller • Lillian Hellman • Beth Henley
John Irving • Randall Jarrell • Charles Johnson • Adrienne Kennedy
William Kennedy • Jack Kerouac • Jamaica Kincaid
Tony Kushner • Ursula K. Le Guin • Denise Levertov
Bernard Malamud • Bobbie Ann Mason • Jill McCorkle
Carson McCullers • W. S. Merwin • Arthur Miller
Toni Morrison's Fiction • Vladimir Nabokov • Gloria Naylor
Joyce Carol Oates • Tim O'Brien • Flannery O'Connor
Cynthia Ozick • Walker Percy • Katherine Anne Porter
Richard Powers • Reynolds Price • Annie Proulx
Thomas Pynchon • Theodore Roethke • Philip Roth
May Sarton • Hubert Selby, Jr. • Mary Lee Settle • Neil Simon
Isaac Bashevis Singer • Jane Smiley • Gary Snyder
William Stafford • Anne Tyler • Kurt Vonnegut
David Foster Wallace • Robert Penn Warren • James Welch
Eudora Welty • Tennessee Williams • August Wilson • Charles Wright

UNDERSTANDING
T. C.
BOYLE

Paul Gleason

The University of South Carolina Press

Published by the University of South Carolina Press
Columbia, South Carolina 29208

www.sc.edu/uscpress

Manufactured in the United States of America

18 17 16 15 14 13 12 11 10 09   10 9 8 7 6 5 4 3 2 1

Library of Congress Cataloging-in-Publication Data

Gleason, Paul William, 1973–
    Understanding T. C. Boyle / Paul Gleason.
        p. cm. — (Understanding contemporary American literature)
    Includes bibliographical references and index.
    ISBN 978-1-57003-780-1 (cloth : alk. paper)
    1. Boyle, T. Coraghessan—Criticism and interpretation. I. Title.
    II. Series.
    PS3552.O932Z67 2009
    813'.54—dc22

                                                          2008042031

The author would like to acknowledge the work of Melissa R. Brooks on
the index.

Contents

Series Editor's Preface

The volumes of *Understanding Contemporary American Literature* have been planned as guides or companions for students as well as good nonacademic readers. The editor and publisher perceive a need for these volumes because much of the influential contemporary literature makes special demands. Uninitiated readers encounter difficulty in approaching works that depart from the traditional forms and techniques of prose and poetry. Literature relies on conventions, but the conventions keep evolving; new writers form their own conventions—which in time may become familiar. Put simply, *UCAL* provides instruction in how to read certain contemporary writers—identifying and explicating their material, themes, use of language, point of view, structures, symbolism, and responses to experience.

The word *understanding* in the titles was deliberately chosen. Many willing readers lack an adequate understanding of how contemporary literature works; that is, what the author is attempting to express and the means by which it is conveyed. Although the criticism and analysis in the series have been aimed at a level of general accessibility, these introductory volumes are meant to be applied in conjunction with the works they cover. They do not provide a substitute for the works and authors they introduce, but rather prepare the reader for more profitable literary experiences.

M. J. B.

UNDERSTANDING
T. C. BOYLE

CHAPTER 1

Understanding T. C. Boyle

Thomas John Boyle was born on 2 December 1948 in Peekskill, New York. When he was seventeen years old, he changed his middle name to Coraghessan (pronounced kuh-RAGG-issun), which came from his mother's side of the family and was his attempt to distance himself from his lower-middle-class upbringing and parents, both of whom died of alcoholism-related illnesses before he was thirty. Boyle, who earned poor grades in high school, wanted to major in music and become a jazz saxophone player when he left Peekskill and entered the State University of New York at Potsdam in the fall of 1965. He failed his audition with the music department and instead chose history as a major. "Why history?" he asks in his important autobiographical essay of 1999, "This Monkey, My Back." "I didn't know at the time," he answers, "or I couldn't have defined it, but it had to do with writing. I didn't yet realize it, but I could write, and in history—unlike, say, biology or math—what you did was write essays."[1]

As a college student, Boyle did not attend classes regularly, choosing instead to drum, sing, and play saxophone in a rock-and-roll band. One of the courses that he did attend, however, immediately caught his attention: his sophomore literature class. It was in this course that he discovered the American short-story writer and novelist Flannery O'Connor and "felt a blast of recognition" in her dark comic vision and moral seriousness.[2] Boyle became an enthusiastic reader and independently read the works of some of the twentieth century's greatest writers, including John Updike, Saul Bellow, Albert Camus, and Samuel Beckett. The works of Beckett and other absurdist writers, which he eventually read as a student in a creative writing workshop offered by Professor Krishna Vaid, particularly affected him "because it was readily apparent that their authors were wise guys just like [him]—albeit very sophisticated, very nasty, and very funny wise guys."[3] Inspired by these writers, Boyle wrote his first creative piece for Professor Vaid's class, a comic one-act play called *The Foot*, in which a husband and wife mourn the death of their child, whom an alligator has devoured. When Boyle read the play aloud in class, he experienced his first public triumph as a writer. After hearing the play, Professor Vaid "began to smile and then to grin and chuckle and finally to laugh without constraint." Professor Vaid and Boyle's fellow students applauded after the reading was finished, and Boyle experienced "the sort of exhilaration that only comes from driving the ball over the net and directly into your opponent's face."[4] Boyle eventually graduated from SUNY Potsdam in 1968 with degrees in English and history and shortly thereafter took a job as a high-school English teacher in Peekskill, a position he held to avoid the Vietnam draft until he entered graduate school at the University of Iowa in 1972.

Boyle's college experience and first reading encapsulate what would eventually become the central aesthetic of his fiction, as well as his understanding of the social role of the fiction writer. Fiction, according to Boyle, should be cynical and funny, performative and strange, but, above all, entertaining and fun. In addition, as his famous public readings and the regularly updated blog at his official Web site demonstrate, Boyle thinks that the fiction writer should be a performer and an entertainer who regularly interacts with his audience in public. As a former history major, Boyle also posits that the fiction writer's texts should contextualize his characters in specific eras of American history and use satire as a moral force for the improvement of society. But as Boyle writes in "This Monkey, My Back," his central identity as a fiction writer, the one that informs every word that he writes, is that of the wise guy—that is, the intelligent, funny, and, perhaps even, arrogant and disrespectful smart aleck who makes readers laugh even as he or she teaches them a lesson.

This concept of the fiction writer as wise guy derives in part from Boyle's reading of absurdist writers such as Beckett but also from his formative engagement with great American postmodernist novelists, particularly John Barth, Thomas Pynchon, and Robert Coover. When Boyle was an undergraduate in the late 1960s and a graduate student in the 1970s, Barth, Pynchon, and Coover were publishing their most experimental, influential, encyclopedic, erudite, and, many readers would argue, difficult works. In particular, four of their novels—Barth's *The Sot-Weed Factor* (1960), Pynchon's *V.* (1963) and *Gravity's Rainbow* (1973), and Coover's *The Public Burning* (1977)—inventively combine historical fact and fiction to satirize specific events in American history.

Barth, Pynchon, and Coover are famous wise guys who poke fun at American mythology, politics, and institutions in their long, difficult, and ambitious historical novels. In his fiction Boyle retains their comic spirit and interest in history but makes his work more accessible and entertaining to his readers. Unlike the difficult canonical modernist writers of the first half of the twentieth century—for example, James Joyce, Marcel Proust,

William Faulkner, and Virginia Woolf—and the equally difficult postmodernist writers who followed them in the second half of the twentieth century—Barth, Pynchon, and Coover, of course, but also William Gaddis, William H. Gass, William S. Burroughs, and Joseph McElroy—Boyle constructs plots and characters that are weird but accessible, thought provoking but immediate. In addition, unlike some of the major works of twentieth-century modernist and postmodernist fiction, Boyle's fiction is earnest, using its comedy to provide clear moral messages at the expense of modernist ironic detachment and postmodernist nihilistic humor.

Boyle's interest in writing funny, entertaining, and moral fiction also derives from his reading of another group of writers when he was in the graduate program at the University of Iowa. Deciding to pursue a Ph.D. in English literature, Boyle specialized in British literature of the Victorian period. This meant that just as he was reading the novels of Barth, Pynchon, and Coover, he was also reading the didactic, popular, and moralizing novels of George Eliot, Thomas Hardy, Charlotte and Emily Brontë, Anthony Trollope, William Makepeace Thackeray, and, above all, Charles Dickens.

Dickens influences Boyle's conception of himself as a socially engaged, entertaining, popular, and prolific writer of fiction. In an interview conducted in 1988 (but not published until 1991), Boyle told Elizabeth Adams that he admires Dickens for being "a quintessential artist, one who was a very popular author, and who also wrote brilliantly and well and originally."[5] In a 2000 interview with Judith Handschuh, Boyle acknowledged the Dickens connection to his own work: "Critics and reviewers have compared me with Dickens, and I take that as a compliment . . . I look to writers like Dickens . . . for inspiration."[6]

Boyle learned from Dickens to entertain his readers with dark humor, strange plots, and even stranger characters. Dickens also taught Boyle to use comedy to provide readers with a moral education. The reader's laughter and anger at the ineffective legal and government systems of *Bleak House* and *Little Dorrit* result in a feeling of compassion for the downtrodden and poor, whose happiness and well-being are harmed by those systems. In addition Dickens, who was an actor and spent his last years giving public readings of his most famous works, exemplifies for Boyle the importance of the writer's role as a public figure, as well as his willingness to reach his readers through public appearances. In the Adams interview, Boyle said, "You have to envy [Dickens] his readings, his famous readings. He was the Mick Jagger and all entertainment of his day wrapped up in one."[7] Finally Boyle and Dickens are both highly prolific writers. By the time he turned fifty-eight at the end of 2006, Boyle had published eleven novels and more than one hundred and fifty short stories.

When Boyle was reading postmodern and Victorian fiction at the University of Iowa, he was also attending the university's Writers' Workshop, where he studied with the important American writers John Irving, Raymond Carver, and John Cheever. Carver and Cheever had a particular—and surprising—impact on Boyle. One of the most important practitioners of literary minimalism, a movement that is characterized by an economic deployment of words and a focus on surface description, Carver inspired Boyle as a graduate student to abandon temporarily the encyclopedic aesthetic of Barth and Pynchon to concentrate on short fiction, a decision that eventually led to the publication of Boyle's first collection of stories, *Descent of Man*, in 1979. This collection disciplined Boyle to condense his dark comic vision and verbal pyrotechnics to the space of individual short stories.

Cheever, on the other hand, provided Boyle with necessary advice. In "This Monkey, My Back," Boyle remembers that Cheever "couldn't make any sense out of *The Sot-Weed Factor* and didn't see that it was worth the effort trying." Cheever taught Boyle that "all good fiction is experimental . . . and don't get caught up in fads."[8] Boyle learned from Cheever to harness his experimental impulses and love of postmodern fiction and write texts that appeal to a large audience through an emphasis on plot and character.

After submitting the *Descent of Man* collection as his creative dissertation in 1977, Boyle graduated from the University of Iowa with a Ph.D. in Victorian literature. In 1978 he accepted an assistant professorship in the English department of the University of Southern California, where he has taught ever since.

The best way to read the work of this self-professed wise guy is to remember its origins in the mind of a man who came of age in the tumultuous decade of the 1960s. Like many members of his generation, T. C. Boyle (he stopped using Coraghessan on his book covers when he published an omnibus collection of his short stories, *T. C. Boyle Stories*, in 1998) as a young man resisted the authority of the establishment, experimented with drugs, rock music, avant-garde literature, and radical ideas, and avoided the Vietnam draft. Some of Boyle's best and best-known fiction—the short story "Greasy Lake" (1981) and the novels *World's End* (1987), *The Tortilla Curtain* (1995), and *Drop City* (2003)—explore his generation from many perspectives, always searching for the motivations for idealism in individual lives and the results of this idealism on American society and history.

Elsewhere in his fiction, Boyle extends his analysis of idealism to other eras of American history. *The Road to Wellville* (1993) and *The Inner Circle* (2004) combine fact and fiction in their explorations of the lives of historical American reformers who have a passionate commitment to changing society for the better and who obsessively and irrationally pursue their quests. *The Road to Wellville* examines Dr. John Harvey Kellogg's attempts at the beginning of the twentieth century to change the eating and exercising habits of Americans in an effort to extend their life spans, presenting the megalomania and fanaticism that existed alongside Kellogg's idealism. *The Inner Circle*, Boyle's novel on the activities of the sex researcher Dr. Alfred Kinsey in the 1930s through the 1950s, works the same thematic territory as *The Road to Wellville*, simultaneously admiring Kinsey for the openness that he brought to American sexuality and deploring him for the harm that his sexual theories caused his family and the members of his research team. In these two historical novels, Boyle concludes that hypocrisy and autocratic authoritarianism reside at the heart of much idealism and many reformist movements. As Boyle himself said in an interview with David L. Ulin, "As an iconoclast and punk who never really grew up . . . I can't stand the idea of authority, and I think it's detrimental to the character of people to give themselves over blindly to authority."[9]

In addition to considering the ramifications of idealism, Boyle's fiction also takes up specific social and political issues. Many of Boyle's novels and short stories consider the relationship between humanity and nature. The marijuana farmers of Boyle's second novel, *Budding Prospects* (1984), get injured when they fight a forest fire that threatens to destroy their illegal crop. A similar fire threatens to destroy the residents of Arroyo Blanco Estates, a fictional community just outside of Los Angeles, in *The Tortilla Curtain*. The unforgiving cold of an Alaskan winter endangers the lives of the residents of a hippie commune in *Drop City*. In *A Friend of the Earth* (2000), an aging environmentalist and hippie experiences the devastating effects of global warming on the earth's biosphere in the year 2025. And Boyle's most recent short-story collections, *After the Plague* (2001) and *Tooth and Claw* (2005), present nature as a violent force that menaces humanity.

Illegal immigration and racism are other key issues that inform Boyle's fiction, especially the novels *East Is East* (1990) and *The Tortilla Curtain*. Both novels discuss the ways in which political theory and personal actions intersect in the lives of characters. *East Is East* considers the interactions of a primarily liberal contingent of authors living in Georgia and the local police and government authorities who apprehend an illegal alien from Japan hiding in the local swamps and cottages. Boyle's text exposes the hypocrisies of both the writers and the authorities. Boyle employs this same method of exposure in *The Tortilla Curtain*, showing how formerly idealistic characters surrender their beliefs in equal human rights as they construct a wall around their wealthy community to deter the entrance of illegal Mexican immigrants. The hypocrisies of the Americans in both texts emphasize underlying racist attitudes that lead to suffering and, ultimately, death.

A final theme that characterizes much of Boyle's fiction concerns the ways in which popular culture helps construct the identities of characters. Boyle's characters are very concerned with their book and record collections, especially the hippies of *Drop City*, who listen to such musicians as Hank Williams, Sonny Rollins, and Jimi Hendrix, read such writers as Julio Cortázar and Hermann Hesse, and name one of their dogs after a character from J. R. R. Tolkien's *The Lord of the Rings*. For Boyle these musicians and writers define the zeitgeist of late-1960s and early-1970s America, so he refers to their works to create his characters in *Drop City*. His other novels use music, literature, and other elements of pop culture in the same way, with even the eighteenth-century characters of *Water Music* (1981) humming catchy songs and attending public concerts.

Two other defining characteristics of Boyle's fiction are his prose style and comic sensibility. Ever since the publication of *Descent of Man* in 1979, critics have remarked on the energy, verve, and highly stylized quality of his prose. In an interview with Patricia Lamberti, Boyle claimed that "language is the key to stories that are purely comic. They are serious because they have underpinnings in extraordinary language."[10] The first sentence of Boyle's first novel, *Water Music*, illustrates the salient features of his prose style: "At an age when most young Scotsmen were lifting skirts, plowing furrows and spreading seed, Mungo Park was displaying his bare buttocks to the al-haj' Ali Ibn Fatoudi, Emir of Ludamar."[11] By presenting his characters in this way, Boyle intensifies the feeling that they exist primarily as linguistic creations and not as real people. Boyle's prose, then, enhances the effect of his characters as vehicles for his satire, social commentaries, and comedy.

Boyle is a great comic writer in his short stories and novels, not just in his style, but also in his outlandish plots. Many of Boyle's detractors have accused him of not constructing plots in his short stories at all but rather comic routines that function primarily as jokes. These detractors emphasize Boyle's comic tales and ignore his morally serious stories, such as "Greasy Lake," "If the River Was Whiskey," "The Fog Man," "Sinking House," and "Rara Avis." Yet there is something of the showman about Boyle in his comic stories. He experiences such public adulation and enjoys a strong base of devoted readers because many of his stories *are* funny. The paranoid hero of "Modern Love" has a lover who wears a full-body condom to prevent the spread of sexually transmitted diseases. A character named T. C. Boyle in "I Dated Jane Austen" takes the author of *Pride and Prejudice* and *Emma* out on the town. The disaffected young narrator of "Beat" goes on a pilgrimage to visit Jack Kerouac at his home, only to find out that the rebel-hero of the Beat Generation lives with his mother. And the hero of "56–0" plays outfield in a seemingly endless—and pointless—baseball game. The origins of these fantastic plots can be found in Boyle's reading of Latin American magical realist writers, such as Julio Cortázar, Jorge Luis Borges, and Gabriel García Márquez, as well as in his engagement with Dickens, Barth, and Pynchon.

But, for the most part Boyle's novels embed their bizarre occurrences in more conventionally realistic plots. *Budding Prospects* provides a good example of how this embedding process works. The main, realistic plot of the novel concerns a group of aging hippies and their attempt to grow marijuana for profit on an illegal farm. The novel, however, occasionally loses touch with realism when strange events happen to the characters.

Boyle's stories and novels take the best elements of Carver's minimalism, Barth's postmodern extravaganzas, García Márquez's magical realism, O'Connor's dark comedy and moral seriousness, and Dickens's entertaining and strange plots and bring them to bear on American life in an accessible, subversive, and inventive way. There is no one quite like Boyle writing in America today. But even as Boyle takes a cynical attitude toward institutions and the men who lead them, even as he thunders for racial tolerance, environmental awareness, and gender equality, he cannot help but convey his love for his characters and, above all, for his audience. Love, then, is the overriding emotion that prevails in Boyle's work—love for language, love for all forms of artistic expression, love for sex and food, love for laughter, and, most important, love for an America that could be so much better.

CHAPTER 2

T. C. Boyle's Short Fiction

An Overview from *Descent of Man* to *Tooth and Claw*

T. C. Boyle has published around one hundred and fifty short stories in literary magazines and eight collections of short fiction in just over a quarter century of writing. He is one of American short fiction's most wide-ranging and adventurous writers. His short fiction consists of political satires ("Ike and Nina" and "The New Moon Party"), takeoffs on and sequels to the works of other writers such as Ernest Hemingway ("Me Cago en la Leche [Robert Jordan in Nicaragua]") and Nikolai Gogol ("The Overcoat II"), autobiographical meditations on small-town America and alcoholic parents ("If the River Was Whiskey" and "Rara Avis"), yarns of romance and sex ("Modern Love" and "Without a Hero"), tales of environmentalism and ecology ("Whales Weep" and "Rapture of the Deep"), comic riffs on American pop culture ("The Hit Man" and "All Shook Up"), and sports writing ("56–0" and "The Hector Quesadilla Story"). To these stories Boyle's two most recent collections, *After the Plague* (2001) and *Tooth and Claw* (2005), append a postapocalyptic analysis of American society ("After the Plague"), complex commentaries on romantic relationships ("She Wasn't Soft" and "Tooth and Claw"), and disturbing studies of controversial American social issues such as drug use and abortion ("Killing Babies" and "Up against the Wall").

Doubletakes: Pairs of Contemporary Short Stories, an anthology of short fiction that Boyle edited and published in 2003, allows the reader to examine and better understand Boyle's own short fiction as a thematic and aesthetic whole.[1] Boyle includes in the anthology stories by many of his key influences: Jorge Luis Borges, Gabriel García Márquez, Robert Coover, and Donald Barthelme. These stories and stories by younger writers such as Aimee Bender, George Saunders, and David Foster Wallace show Boyle's debt to and interest in magical realism and experimental fiction in general. Boyle's short fiction grows out of his interest in experimental writers but also comes from his engagement with three other writers whose stories he includes in the anthology. From John Cheever and Raymond Carver, his two mentors at the University of Iowa Writers' Workshop, Boyle learns to create mainly unexceptional white middle- to lower-middle-class male protagonists for whom contemporary American life affords seemingly endless angst and boredom. In addition Cheever's thematic interest in questioning ethical behavior in a morally ambiguous society, along with Carver's minimalism, influences many of Boyle's stories. And Flannery O'Connor, the author of Boyle's favorite short story, "A Good Man Is Hard to Find," teaches Boyle to use dark humor to deliver strong moral messages in his short fiction. Boyle commented on O'Connor's impact on his work in an interview with Patricia Lamberti: "She was very satiric and kept a jaundiced eye on her society. She taught me about taking a microscopic lens and turning it on society."[2]

Doubletakes also incorporates many direct statements on Boyle's theory of short fiction, which emphasizes entertainment as the first goal of the short-story writer and reader: "My aesthetic, as a writer and reader both, is to elevate the sense of enjoyment above all other literary considerations, to remind us all that literature is an art and that art exists to entertain" (vii–viii). Boyle stresses the role of voice in entertaining the reader: "Narrative voice is the beginning, and voice controls the mode of the story—i.e., will this be narrated in the first, second, or third person and how will the tone color it—and gives rise to all the rest: development of character, theme, language, structure, and symbology" (viii). In choosing pairs of short stories by individual writers and not the normal single story, Boyle allows the readers of *Doubletakes* to consider the ways in which writers use entertainment and voice to develop their thematic interests over the course of multiple works.

This chapter on Boyle's short fiction employs the same method that Boyle adopts in choosing stories for *Doubletakes*. After giving a brief thematic overview of each of Boyle's six collections of previously uncollected short fiction (*T. C. Boyle Stories* and the 2005 collection, *The Human Fly,* are not included because they mainly include previously published stories), each section of this chapter presents two stories from each collection. By pairing a comedy and a more somber work from each collection, this chapter provides a detailed account of the themes and aesthetic concerns that characterize individual volumes of Boyle's short fiction, traces his development as a short-story writer, and explores his short fiction in relation to his novels.

Descent of Man: Stories (1979)

Containing mainly short stories that Boyle wrote as a graduate student and published in literary magazines in the early-to-mid 1970s, *Descent of Man* is his first published book, his Ph.D. thesis, and the winner of the 1980 St. Lawrence Award for Short Fiction. The title of the collection comes from Charles Darwin's second book on evolutionary theory, *The Descent of Man* (1871). Darwin's book applies his theory of natural selection, which he originally outlined in *The Origin of Species* (1859), to human evolution, sexuality, psychology, ethics, and race. In Darwin's own words, the purpose of *The Descent of Man* "is to consider, firstly, whether man, like every other species, is descended from some pre-existing form; secondly, the manner of his development; and thirdly, the value of the differences between the so-called races of men."[3]

Like Darwin, Boyle in *Descent of Man* blurs the boundary between the rational or spiritual human world and the irrational animal world. In an interview with Nathan Leslie, Boyle said, "I'm very conscious of trying to see what the boundary between the animal and the spiritual or mental is in our lives."[4] But whereas Darwin's theory that natural selection applies both to animals and humans had devastating epistemological, philosophical, and theological implications for nineteenth-century readers, Boyle's collection refers to Darwin's text to satirize a so-called enlightened humanity that thinks itself more rationally advanced than the animal world. As Denis Hennessy has argued, "*Descent of Man* . . . displays Boyle's overriding theme: the unavoidable reversion of humankind to prelapsarian animality, a state of being characterized by physical coarseness and the absence of conscience."[5] Funny but slight stories such as "The Champ," "Heart of a Champion," "We Are Norsemen," and "Bloodfall" mine this theme for comic effect, whereas a pair of stories from the collection, "Descent of Man" and "Drowning," more successfully and complexly conveys Boyle's satire.

Boyle argues in *Doubletakes* that the first line of a story both establishes its voice and "sets the table" for the entertainment that follows (3). The first line of "Descent of Man" is as follows:

"I was living with a woman who suddenly began to stink."[6] The reader soon learns that the woman in question, Jane Good, works in a primate center as an animal behaviorist and has a close relationship with a very intelligent chimpanzee named Konrad, who spends his days reading Yerkish translations of Noam Chomsky and Friedrich Nietzsche. The name "Jane Good" is, of course, a thinly veiled reference to Jane Goodall, the ethologist who lived with and studied chimpanzees in the wilds of Tanzania, and the name "Konrad" refers to Joseph Conrad, the modernist author whose novella *Heart of Darkness* reveals the irrational desires that reside at the heart of the nominally rational enterprises of Europeans. The story recounts the love triangle that develops among Jane, Konrad, and Horne, the frustrated narrator, with Jane's lack of personal hygiene demonstrating her reversion—or descent—to Konrad's state of animality. "Descent of Man" concludes with Horne arriving at the primate center to find Jane, who has moved out of the home that she shares with him, and Konrad "experimenting" with sexual intercourse. Konrad, who physically intimidates Horne with his "black eyes, teeth, fur, rock-ribbed arms" (105), wins the primeval contest for sexual superiority.

Boyle's satire in "Descent of Man" operates on two important levels. First, it parodies the concept of enlightened and rational humanity. Jane's objective science fails when she becomes sexually attracted to Konrad, and Horne cannot use his rational faculties to account for Jane's defection to the arms of the chimpanzee. Boyle's understanding that irrational and so-called primitive desires underlie humanity's actions forms the story's central message, which resembles the theme of Conrad's *Heart of Darkness*. But Boyle's postmodern text employs parody and comedy to make fun of not just humanity's essential primitivism but also modernism's earnest and solemn attempt to aestheticize that primitivism in, for example, the works of Matisse, Stravinsky, Picasso, and D. H. Lawrence. "Descent of Man" contains a comic self-awareness that is foreign to Conrad's novella and these other canonical artworks of modernism.

"Drowning," the final story in *Descent of Man*, approaches the collection's overriding theme of human animality from a tragic perspective. Denis Hennessy indicates that "Drowning" and many of Boyle's other closing stories "have been chosen to summarize and emphasize his major theme."[7] In the story Boyle abandons the antic comedy and satire that characterize many of the preceding stories and appropriates a more modernist approach to present his central theme. Like such modernists as James Joyce, Virginia Woolf, and William Faulkner, Boyle narrates the central dramatic events of his story from multiple perspectives. These perspectives include that of a young woman who sunbathes in the nude on an isolated beach, that of a man who rapes her, and that of another man who drowns in the sea while the rape transpires five hundred yards away from him. Boyle develops a parallel relationship between the drowning and the rape to show the extent to which humanity, like nature, is essentially irrational, controlled by primal urges, and dangerous. In addition, as two potential rescuers discover the woman and the rapist on the beach only to rape her themselves, Boyle argues that humanity has not used its rationality to eliminate immoral and unethical deeds.

Greasy Lake and Other Stories (1985)

First published in 1985, Boyle's second collection of short fiction was *Greasy Lake and Other Stories*. In the six years between *Descent of Man* and *Greasy Lake*, Boyle had published his first two novels, *Water Music* (1981) and *Budding Prospects* (1984). *Greasy Lake* most resembles *Budding Prospects*, which satirizes capitalism in its presentation of the adventures of a team of aging California hippies who try to grow an illegal crop of marijuana for profit. Like *Budding Prospects*, the stories collected in *Greasy Lake* explore social issues, such as artificial insemination, the treatment of the elderly, environmentalism, and the relationship between political promises and political actions.

"Greasy Lake,"[8] the title story of the collection, takes the same postmodern approach that Boyle employs in "Descent of Man": it refers to another text in its title, in this case Bruce Springsteen's 1973 song "Spirit in the Night." "Spirit in the Night" celebrates and romanticizes Greasy Lake as an escape from the constraints of conventional American life and as a place where drug use and sex lead to spiritual enlightenment.

Boyle begins his "Greasy Lake" with an epigraph taken from Springsteen's song that indicates the location of Greasy Lake: "It's about a mile down on the dark side of Route 88" (261). His story portrays the dark side of thinking that rebellious drug use and sex result in spiritual enlightenment. For Boyle the first line of the story is, as usual, instrumental in setting up the story's theme: "There was a time when courtesy and winning ways went out of style, when it was good to be bad, when you cultivated decadence like a taste" (261). The narrator of the story immediately establishes himself as an older man reflecting on the vanished days of his youth, when being a social rebel was acceptable. He and his friends, Digby and Jeff, strike "elaborate poses to show that [they] didn't give a shit about anything," but they are really just mild-mannered college students who enjoy the monetary support of their parents (261).

The toughness of the narrator and his friends is put to the test when they visit Greasy Lake one night. Already drunk and stoned by the time they reach the lake, they see what they think is the car of their friend Tony Lovett but soon learn that the car actually belongs to a "very bad character in greasy jeans and engineer boots" who is making out with his girlfriend (262–63). After the narrator ends the ensuing fight by hitting the bad character, Bobby, in the head with a tire iron, he and his friends attempt to rape the girlfriend but are interrupted by an approaching car. The narrator flees to the woods, where he wades into a pond and discovers a decaying corpse.

Not Springsteen's place of mystical escape, Boyle's Greasy Lake is a site of violence and death. The narrator's comparison between his and his friends' decision to approach Bobby's car and "Westmoreland's decision to dig in at Khe Sanh" links the events that transpire at Greasy Lake to the conflict in Vietnam, which many Americans opposed on moral and political grounds (262). As college students, Digby, Jeff, and the narrator are not eligible for the draft, so the narrator's comparison highlights their personal immaturity, which does not allow them to recognize their status as economically privileged members of society. Unlike many of their poorer contemporaries who have to fight in the jungles of Vietnam, the narrator and his friends have the privilege of constructing themselves as "bad" characters. As Michael Walker has argued, the friends "are unwitting soldiers in a Vietnam of their own making, out of their depth."[9] When Boyle's narrator finds the corpse in the pond in the woods, the reader realizes the mortality and animality that connect all humans and morally condemns the narrator and his friends for their violent actions.

"All Shook Up," another story from the *Greasy Lake* collection, is the story of an unsuccessful Elvis Presley impersonator, and like "Greasy Lake," it explores the relationship between appearance and identity. Patrick, the twenty-nine-year-old narrator of the story, is a high-school guidance counselor whose wife, Judy, has recently left him. When twenty-year-old Cindy Greco and her twenty-one-year-old husband, Joey, move into the house next door, Patrick immediately notices from Joey's voice and appearance that he is an Elvis impersonator and later agrees to visit their house for dinner. Patrick's musical interests do not include Elvis: "By the time I gave up pellet guns and minibikes and began listening to rock and roll, it was the Doors, Stones, and Hendrix, and Elvis was already degenerating into a caricature of himself" (124). His condescending attitude toward Joey arises from his opinion that by impersonating Elvis, Joey makes a caricature out of a caricature. Patrick's underlying assumption is that musicians such as the Doors, the Rolling Stones, and Jimi Hendrix are more authentic and complex than Elvis Presley.

Boyle uses the rhetoric of authenticity to indicate the ways in which Patrick himself is just as much of an impersonator as Joey. Patrick's job as a high-school guidance counselor affords him the opportunity of giving advice to many attractive and pregnant girls. Patrick admits that he is attracted to these girls, but his position as an authority in the school prevents him from acting on his desires. When Patrick begins an affair with the much younger Cindy, however, the reader sees that his ethics do not impede his sexual desire for much younger women, that he only requires a convenient social situation, like the invitation to dinner. By the conclusion of the story, when Patrick accepts his wife's offer to return home without telling her about the affair, the reader comprehends his unethical nature, hypocritical self-absorption, and immaturity. Patrick does not want the responsibility of caring for Cindy and her baby when Joey offers them to him at the end of the story. Patrick's posturing with Cindy and his wife has greater and more lasting consequences than Joey's more benign Elvis impersonation. Even though "All Shook Up," with Joey's amusing Elvis impersonations, is more comic than "Greasy Lake," it nonetheless critiques the dark behavior of its protagonist.

If the River Was Whiskey: Stories (1989)

If the River Was Whiskey, Boyle's third collection of short fiction, appeared in 1989, four years after *Greasy Lake*, and won the 1989 PEN Center West Literary Prize and was chosen by the editors of the *New York Times Book Review* as one of the thirteen best books of 1989.[10] Two of the collection's best stories, "Sinking House" and "The Ape Lady in Retirement," won O. Henry Awards. During the four years between *Greasy Lake* and *If the River Was Whiskey*, Boyle published in 1987 his first major novel, *World's End*, an encyclopedic work that examines class, race, politics, and other social issues in seventeenth- and twentieth-century New York state. *If the River Was Whiskey* parallels the complex analysis of America in *World's End* because, as Dan Pope has argued, it "reveals and illuminates the distinctive perplexities of the contemporary American experience."[11] As Boyle does in creating Peterskill, New York, as a fictional version of his hometown of Peekskill in *World's End*, he effects this analysis by including autobiography in *If the River Was Whiskey*.

The title story of the collection shows Boyle's willingness to use autobiography to convey real human emotion and not his usual satire and comedy. Like Boyle, Tiller, the young hero of the story, has alcoholic parents who argue all the time and seem on the verge of separation and possible divorce. Tiller spends most of the story, which takes place at a run-down vacation resort in the woods, futilely trying to connect with his disinterested and emotionally detached father. He encounters his father playing guitar and singing "If the River Was Whiskey," an old blues song. When Tiller tries to connect with his father by saying, "I really liked the song, Dad" (232), his father offers him a sip of beer and is unable to communicate the meaning of the song, which concerns the narrator's longing to drown his sorrows in whiskey because his beloved will not return his love. Just as alcohol replaces the loving relationship in the song, it also replaces the loving bond between Tiller and his father in the story. The father's inability to understand—or, at least, to articulate—the meaning of the song indicates his inability to comprehend the importance of his relationship with his son.

The song very explicitly connects whiskey and water, and Boyle's text follows suit. In the penultimate section of the story, Tiller finally manages to convince his father to take a boat trip with him to fish for pike. Boyle employs fishing as a symbol of the search for spiritual growth to offer the possibility that Tiller and his father can achieve a stronger relationship during their excursion. Like Jesus and his disciples in the Bible, Tiller and his father fish the waters, but they do not experience a similar spiritual communion. Tiller's father is at first excited about the prospect of catching a pike, but when the fish do not bite, he dozes in the boat until Tiller notices activity on his line. He reels in the fish, only to find that it is not a pike but a carp, and Tiller feels "like crying" (234). The story concludes with Tiller's father having a drunken dream in which he helplessly watches as his son drowns. This sadly moving ending, which emphasizes the hopelessness and helplessness that both the father and son feel in their relationship, allows Boyle to explore his interest in ineffective communication.

"Sorry Fugu" is perhaps the most successful comic depiction of communication problems in *If the River Was Whiskey*. It recounts the adventures of Albert, a young and ambitious chef and the owner of an Italian restaurant named D'Angelo's, and his attempts to inspire the overly harsh critic Willa Frank to give him a good review in her "Dining Out" column.[12] The story concerns Albert's attempt to communicate with Willa through the medium of specially prepared meals. He fails in his efforts until he distracts Jock, her dining companion who helps her form her opinions, with a homey meal of "three boiled potatoes, a splatter of reduced peas, and what could only be described as a plank of meat, stiff and flat as the chopping block, black as the bottom of the pan" that he knows Jock will like based on his knowledge of Jock's upbringing (31). When Willa visits the kitchen to demand an explanation for the meal, Albert is finally able to communicate to her without the interference of Jock and solicits a good review by seducing her with squid rings in aioli sauce, lobster tortellini, and other delicacies. In "Sorry Fugu," Boyle illuminates the difficulties individuals have directly communicating with each other and the almost sensual experience of achieving direct communication. By the end of the story, Albert addresses Willa with a "voice soft as a lover's" (33).

Without a Hero: Stories (1994)

As Denis Hennessy has argued, the theme of Boyle's fourth collection of stories, *Without a Hero*, is "the vacuum left by the disappearance of the hero, not only in fiction but in real lives."[13] The two novels that Boyle published between *If the River Was Whiskey* and *Without a Hero*—*East Is East* (1990) and *The Road to Wellville* (1993)—reflect Hennessy's argument and show that Boyle's fiction maintains a thematic consistency throughout this period. The writers and government authorities of *East Is East* do not take a heroic stand and support the rights of Hiro, the ironically named Japanese illegal alien. In *The Road to*

Wellville, Boyle exposes the megalomaniac impulses at the heart of the idealistic and nominally heroic science of Dr. John Harvey Kellogg. The best and most memorable stories of *Without a Hero* also consider the disappearance of the hero from many stylistic angles. "Beat" employs Boyle's traditional dark comic approach to reveal the superficial aspects of Jack Kerouac's rebellious heroism. In addition the reader of "The Fog Man" sees its main character in a negative light for not defending the rights of a Japanese-American girl whom his best friend and classmates harass. In "Without a Hero," moreover, Boyle's narrator and his Russian immigrant lover take advantage of each other to advance their personal selfish desires, his sexual and hers materialistic.

One of the collection's best stories, "Filthy with Things," tells the story of Susan Certaine, a professional organizer, and her attempt to organize the myriad useless material possessions that make the house of a hapless couple, Julian and Marsha Laxner, an unruly mess.[14] Boyle constructs Certaine as a messianic hero, her last name a pun on the dedication and decisiveness with which she performs the duties of her job. Certaine reveals herself to be a false hero and a domineering presence in the lives of her clients by demanding that Marsha and Julian vacate their home and sending the wife to a rehabilitation hostel for people who compulsively make needless purchases and the husband to "The Co-Dependent Hostel. For spouses" (685). When Julian questions Certaine's authority, escapes the hostel, and holes up in a nondescript motel, Certaine inexplicably knows where to find him, telephoning him to order him to return to the hostel. Like a comic Big Brother, Certaine wields omniscient power over the lives of her clients.

Boyle directs his satire in "Filthy with Things" at American capitalist society as a whole. Both the Laxners and Susan Certaine illustrate the extent to which the purchasing of commodities constitutes the primary drive of American life. Boyle uses Marsha's sickness as a means of satirizing this drive as typically American. Only in the affluence of American society, Boyle suggests, can the attainment of commodities become an illness. In addition Boyle satirizes the ways in which Americans design jobs for experts to help people manage their largely self-created problems. Certaine, like the new-age gurus and life coaches of contemporary America, exists only because of American privilege and greed. At the end of this story, she herself emphasizes this privilege and greed not by organizing the possessions in the Laxners' home but by having them removed to be redistributed according to the dictates of Certaine Enterprises, Inc. Despite Certaine's assertion to Julian that some of the possessions may be sold at auction for charity, the reader realizes that part of her motivation in working as a professional organizer is to gain control of her clients' belongings.

One of Boyle's most complex and emotionally powerful stories, "Sitting on Top of the World," is the final story in *Without a Hero*. The protagonist of the story is a thirty-something woman named Lainie, who works for the Forestry Service as a fire watcher in a glass tower in the Sierras. Separated from her husband, Lainie is an ascetic spending her summer away from humanity and experiencing the healing powers of the natural world. Lainie's meditations on her separation from her husband and her relationship with her son reveal both her strong independence as a woman and her loneliness and need for human contact. When a mysterious male interloper begins visiting her repeatedly in her tower and indicates his attraction to her, Lainie reacts with annoyance, fear, and fascination. Boyle is ambiguous about the interloper's motive so that he can explore Lainie's character through the complexities of her at times contradictory reactions. When the interloper makes a fire in the woods to attract Lainie's attention, Boyle writes, "Then [Lainie] propped herself in the corner of the bed, way out over the edge of the abyss, and watched his fire raging in the cold heart of the night. He would be back, she knew that now, and she would be ready for him" (227). Like Boyle's characterization of the interloper, this ending is deliberately indefinite, requiring the reader to decide whether Lainie will accept the interloper's advances or defend herself with her knife.

Boyle makes a parallel between Lainie and Sleeping Beauty, the fairy-tale heroine who pricks her finger on a magic spindle and falls asleep in an enchanted castle, only to be awakened by the kiss of a handsome prince. The fairy tale characterizes Sleeping Beauty as a helpless woman and the prince as a powerful hero, granting the two figures clearly defined roles based on gender. Boyle's story complicates these gender roles. At the end of the story, the reader remains uncertain about the interloper's motivation and Lainie's reaction to his advances. Because people ultimately do not know the motivations of other individuals, they cannot easily recognize heroism and may wonder whether it actually exists.

After the Plague and Other Stories (2001)

Boyle published *After the Plague*, his fifth collection of short stories, in 2001. Two of the collection's best stories, "The Underground Gardens" and "The Love of My Life," won O. Henry Awards. Another story, "Killing Babies," was included in the

1997 *Best American Stories*. In the seven years between collections, he published three novels—*The Tortilla Curtain* (1995), *Riven Rock* (1998), and *A Friend of the Earth* (2000)—and an omnibus edition of his first four volumes of stories, *T. C. Boyle Stories* (1998), that adds seven previously uncollected tales. Boyle's winning of the 1999 PEN/Malamud Award for Short Fiction for *T. C. Boyle Stories* demonstrates the high regard in which the critical establishment holds his stories. Moreover *T. C. Boyle Stories* serves as an important turning point in the career of its author. The novels of this period and the stories collected in *After the Plague* are, for the most part, more somber in tone, present a darker comic vision of American life, and comment more directly on social issues. *The Tortilla Curtain* exposes the racist attitudes that affect many Americans' opposition to Mexican immigration; *Riven Rock* explores American society's negative response to the early feminists and the mentally ill; and *A Friend of the Earth* presents a horrific future America destroyed by environmental irresponsibility. Many of the key stories in *After the Plague* mine similar social issues as the novels, including abortion and the sexual objectification of women.

"She Wasn't Soft" and "After the Plague," two of the stories in *After the Plague*, demonstrate the ways in which Boyle uses dark comedy to comment on American social issues.[15] "She Wasn't Soft," which Boyle so highly esteems that he included it in his *Doubletakes* anthology, is the tale of Paula Turk, a twenty-eight-year-old triathlete, and Jason Barre, a "thirty-three-year-old surf-and-dive shop proprietor she'd been seeing pretty steadily over the past nine months" (21). On the surface a story about the personality conflict between Paula and Jason, the text is also a meditation on the status of women in contemporary American society. The story centers on Paula's desire to defeat her archrival, Zinny Bauer, in an upcoming triathlon. With Boyle describing the way in which Paula prepares for the competition by visiting a restaurant called the Pasta Bowl with Jason for a "carbo-load" (24), the story begins as one of his comedies. The mood of the story turns dark when Jason rapes Paula after she, wanting to conserve her energy for the triathlon, refuses him sex. By switching rapidly from a comic tone to a description of a shocking event, Boyle disorients the reader and highlights the potential for violence that exists in any relationship. In an interview with Patricia Lamberti, Boyle commented on this technique of switching from a comic to serious tone: "My comic stories contain very serious messages about our society. What I like best . . . is to combine the two to make a tragic, yet wild, off-the-wall tale. That way the story catches you by surprise."[16] Boyle's serious message in "She Wasn't Soft" is that despite their advances in social equality, contemporary American women are still demeaned by men as sexual objects.

The concluding story of *After the Plague*, the collection's title story, corresponds to the postapocalyptic tales of science-fiction writers and illustrates Boyle's notion that, as he said in an interview at the Web site *Failbetter*, "We are all imminently doomed."[17] The thirty-five-year-old narrator of the story, Francis Xavier Halloran III, is a high-school social-studies teacher at a college preparatory institution in Santa Barbara who takes a year-long sabbatical to live in a cabin in the Sierras. His isolation allows him to escape the "Ebola mutation [that] passed from hand to hand and nose to nose like the common cold" and kills most of the earth's population (281). Boyle mines Halloran's matter-of-fact voice for comic effect, inspiring the reader to laugh at the mundane tone with which Halloran recounts his response to the devastating events that led to demise of millions of people. Halloran's reaction to the arrival of a woman named Sarai exemplifies this mundane tone. When Sarai passionately yells, "Open the goddamned door! Help, for shit's sake, help!" (287), Halloran, the "cautious animal" (287), neither rejoices at the prospect of a communion with another human nor leaps to help her; rather, he fears that by opening the door he "would invite the pestilence in and that three days hence both she and [he] would be reduced to [their] mortal remains" (287). After Halloran and Sarai finally meet, Boyle satirizes the former for his inability to comfort her when she grieves over the loss of her boyfriend Howard and for his cold request that they have sex to start the process of repopulating the species and satirizes the latter for being unable to admit that the plague has destroyed most of the earth's population. Like "She Wasn't Soft," "After the Plague" considers power relationships between the genders, but it offers a more specific analysis of the ways in which ineffective communication helps form these power relationships.

The second half of "After the Plague," after Halloran and Sarai separate, offers a disturbing commentary on gender relations. Having moved back to his house outside Santa Barbara, Halloran visits a grocery store, where he discovers Felicia, a teller from his bank. The two plague survivors soon begin a romance, with Halloran commenting that the heavy Felicia "was a relief after stringy Sarai" (298). Halloran goes on to say that Felicia "was decent and kind, sweet even, and more important, she was available" (298). Halloran's shallowness underlies the edenic imagery that characterizes the "new world, "new beginning," and prelapsarian nudity of his life with Felicia (300), illuminating its essential ethical hollowness. Unlike the biblical flood, Boyle's plague does not rid humanity of its sins; rather, it perpetuates them. Halloran's final misdeed is to reunite Howard and Sarai, thereby condemning Howard to experience the same difficulties with her that he had.

Tooth and Claw and Other Stories (2005)

In 2005 Boyle published his sixth volume of short fiction, *Tooth and Claw*, which collects the stories that he wrote between 2001 and 2005. During the same time period, Boyle also published two critically acclaimed novels—*Drop City* (2003) and *The Inner Circle* (2004). The collection covers a wide range of topics, which Boyle renders with his usual flair for dark comedy and absurd plots. "Tooth and Claw," included in the 2004 *Best American Stories*, presents a young man's simultaneous attempts to care for a feral African cat and woo a young woman; "Dogology" pairs the story of a young suburban woman who runs wild with a pack of stray dogs in her neighborhood and a tale of feral children in India; and "When I Woke Up This Morning, Everything I Had Was Gone" chronicles the grief that a father feels for his son, who dies during a night of binge drinking at a fraternity.

A pair of stories, "The Kind Assassin" and "Up against the Wall," presents the central styles and themes of *Tooth and Claw*.[18] Like "She Wasn't Soft" and many of the other tales in *After the Plague*, "The Kind Assassin" employs dark comedy to comment on gender relations. But Boyle extends the scope of "The Kind Assassin" to see gender relations in the light of popular culture. In the story Boomer is a morning disk jockey who works for a California radio station named KFUN and attempts to set the world record for continuous hours without sleep. KFUN publicizes Boomer's attempt, building a small Plexiglas studio for him on a busy street so that his fans can monitor his progress. Boyle creates this absurd situation to satirize and criticize an American popular culture that relies on spectacle and human suffering for entertainment.

Boyle is interested in how Boomer's ordeal affects his relationships with women. Hezza, a twenty-something woman who is younger than Boyle's thirty-something protagonist, adores Boomer as an icon of popular culture and presses a piece of paper with the words "YOU ARE MY GOD" to one of the Plexiglas walls of his studio (65). With Boomer suffering the effects of extreme sleep deprivation, he invites Hezza into his studio for moral and physical support, eventually taking her to his private bathroom, where he demands that she take off her clothes so that they can have sex. Even though the sex does not happen, Boomer's request encourages the reader to question the ethical implications of power relations between genders in the story. Boyle's depiction of Hezza's love for Boomer—she holds up another sign that reads "I LOVE YOU" (77)—appears to suggest that the disk jockey and his fan achieve a true emotional bond. But Boyle complicates the reader's perception of this "love," not just in the scene in the bathroom, but also on the story's final page, when Boomer and Hezza arrive at Boomer's apartment to make love after he sets the record. After the love making, he cannot fall asleep, and he seems to see "a figure stepp[ing] out of the mist" who shoots him "between the parietal plates" with a gun (78). Boyle creates an ambiguous ending—the reader does not know if this is Boomer's hallucination, an indication of his craziness, or simply his way of falling asleep—that questions Boomer's sanity and the reality of his love for Hezza.

"Up against the Wall," the final story in *Tooth and Claw*, is another tale of moral complexity. Returning Boyle to the autobiographical mode of stories such as "Rara Avis" and "If the River Was Whiskey," "Up against the Wall" tells the story of twenty-one-year-old John Caddis, a recent college graduate and Peterskill native who lives with his alcoholic parents and teaches "eighth-grade English in a ghetto school" (259). John and Boyle have a lot in common, both finding teaching jobs to avoid the Vietnam draft and experimenting with hard drugs. As Boyle said in a 2005 interview with Robert Birnbaum, the story "goes to a period of [his] life when [he] was 21 and teaching at a school in New York and having some hard times and it is not purely autobiographical but it uses a lot of autobiographical material and it's straightforward."[19] In a 1990 interview with Tad Friend, Boyle was more specific about his drug use during the period, describing himself as "a dilettante of heroin."[20]

In "Up against the Wall," John's job allows him to obtain "a deferment two weeks short of the date [he] was to report for induction into the U.S. Army, with Vietnam vivid on the horizon" (259). As in "Greasy Lake," the Vietnam conflict underlies all the action that follows in the story, as does the sense that John and his disaffected friends knowingly appropriate the style of the counterculture to pose as rebels. John is very aware of the hair length of his male friends, the dress of his female friends, and the popular music to which they listen, and he tries to grow a mustache "because Ringo Starr had one and George Harrison and Eric Clapton and just about anybody else staring out at you from the front cover of a record album" (261). Whereas John's position at his school requires him to slick down his long, kinky hair, which he models on the hairdo of Jimi Hendrix (264), his longing to fit in with his friends inspires him to let his hair flow freely. John is caught between the worlds of conformity and the counterculture, both of which appear equally hollow in the story.

The reader empathizes with John's feeling of confinement within the conventional world of his school and family and his longing to join in the world of the counterculture. When John and his friend Cole venture to a cabin in the woods, in which young hippies drink, smoke pot, and listen to records and live music, Boyle offers a potential escape from conventional society that reminds one of Springsteen's mystical Greasy Lake. As in his story "Greasy Lake," however, Boyle undermines the magic of this hidden place, this time by depicting the escalation of the hippies' drug use from marijuana and alcohol to heroin. After John joins his friends in their experimentation with heroin and becomes an addict, one of his students questions him about the needle marks on his arm. With John's drug habit paralleling his father's alcoholism, he simply reenacts the destructive behavior that he thinks he is leaving behind when he visits his friends in the cabin in the woods. Boyle darkly suggests that these so-called rebels self-destructively imitate the behavior of their conventional parents.

Despite being complex, intriguing, and often extremely funny and provocative on their own terms, Boyle's short stories in many cases also serve as texts in which he first approaches key themes he later explores in more depth in his novels. For instance, "Descent of Man," one of his first stories, introduces the theme of a so-called enlightened humanity's essential irrationality, which *Water Music*, his first novel, explores with greater penetration. "If the River Was Whiskey" demonstrates the autobiographical bent that also characterizes *World's End*; "Filthy with Things" includes a chief character, Susan Certaine, whose megalomania and skewed idealism parallel similar traits in Dr. John Harvey Kellogg in *The Road to Wellville* and Dr. Alfred Kinsey in *The Inner Circle*; and "After the Plague" is a postapocalyptic tale of viral devastation that precedes the environmental disaster in *A Friend of the Earth*. In using his best short stories as "workshops" in which he develops thematic ideas for his novels, Boyle creates a series of exciting intertextual relationships that allow the reader to consider his key issues—American history, the social ramifications of idealism and science, environmentalism, illegal immigration, racism, and the role of popular culture in the formation of identity—from many disparate angles and perspectives.

CHAPTER 3

T. C. Boyle's Novels of the 1980s

Water Music, Budding Prospects, and *World's End*

When T. C. Boyle was a graduate student at the University of Iowa in the 1970s, the American postmodern meganovel was flourishing. In just under ten years, six major American postmodern meganovels appeared: Thomas Pynchon's *Gravity's Rainbow* (1973), Samuel R. Delany's *Dhalgren* (1975), Joseph McElroy's *Lookout Cartridge* (1974), William Gaddis's *J R* (1975), Robert Coover's *The Public Burning* (1977), and John Barth's *LETTERS* (1979). The critic Frederick R. Karl has characterized these postmodern meganovels as long, difficult, and encyclopedic works that respond to post–World War II and cold-war America, criticize traditional American assumptions and ideologies, and satirize such American institutions as the armed forces, the military industrial complex, Wall Street, Hollywood, higher education, and the Republican Party. With "the 60s spirit as a hovering presence," these works are dark, cynical, and, with the exception of *Dhalgren* and *Lookout Cartridge*, extremely funny.[1] In addition these postmodern meganovels are metafictional—that is, they self-consciously address the devices of fiction.

Pynchon, McElroy, Coover, and Barth were all born in the 1930s, and Gaddis was born in the 1920s. Only Delany shares Boyle's birth decade of the 1940s. Except for Delany, the writers of Boyle's generation for the most part reject the principles of the postmodern meganovel in favor of minimalism. Boyle's contemporaries—writers such as Raymond Carver, Richard Ford, Tobias Wolff, Ann Beattie, and Jayne Anne Phillips—write fiction that shuns the experimental and, some would argue, difficult techniques of the postmodern meganovelist in favor of fiction that portrays the everyday lives of ordinary and sometimes socially marginalized Americans. By using a simple vocabulary and more conventional structures and syntactical patterns, the minimalists deemphasize formal innovations and concentrate instead on a direct depiction of realistic characters responding to social and economic realities. The first examples of minimalism were published at the same time that the postmodern meganovel was at its height: Carver's *Will You Please Be Quiet, Please?* (1976), *Furious Seasons* (1977), and *What We Talk about When We Talk about Love* (1981); Ford's *A Piece of My Heart* (1976) and *The Ultimate Good Luck* (1981); Wolff's *In the Garden of the North American Martyrs* (1981); Beattie's *Distortions* (1976) and *Secrets and Surprises* (1978); and Phillips's *Sweethearts* (1976), *Counting* (1978), and *Black Tickets* (1979).

Boyle's novels of the 1980s incorporate the stylistic strategies and thematic concerns of both the postmodern meganovel and minimalist fiction. Boyle adopts the satiric, cynical, metafictional, and comedic tendencies of the postmodern meganovel but avoids the extreme length and intense self-reflexivity that can make these works difficult to read and compromise the believability of their characters. Like Carver and his followers, Boyle creates realistic characters that come from specific cultures and economic classes, but his outlandish comic plots and mannered prose style do not adhere to the tenets of minimalism. Boyle's early novels—*Water Music*, *Budding Prospects*, and

World's End—can be read as amalgams of the postmodern and minimalist fictions that were in ascendancy when he began publishing in the early 1980s. Boyle acknowledged this amalgamation in an interview with Nathan Leslie: "I would like to be remembered as someone who bridged the writers of the late sixties and early seventies [Pynchon, Barth, and Coover] and the realist writers of the eighties [Carver, Wolff, and Ford], someone who created a kind of fusion and did something a little different and pointed in another direction."[2]

Water Music (1981)

T. C. Boyle's first novel, *Water Music*, is a historical novel of eighteenth-century exploration and adventure that pays homage to the picaresque tales of Henry Fielding and Charles Dickens and to John Barth's metafictional foray into the eighteenth-century novel, *The Sot-Weed Factor*. Many of Boyle's first reviewers praised *Water Music* for its verbal dexterity, exciting plot, antic comedy, and originality, with one critic comparing it to Steven Spielberg's movie *Raiders of the Lost Ark* as a gripping tale of adventure.[3] Boyle does entertain in *Water Music* by populating the book with memorable and strange characters and filling its plot with cliff-hangers, twists and turns, and melodramatic moments. But *Water Music* is not just a ripping good yarn; it is also a metafictional commentary on the picaresque form, the Age of Reason, and social class. Much like Salman Rushdie's *Midnight's Children*, the other great metafictional, picaresque, and comic historical novel of 1981, *Water Music* critiques the violent imperialism and racism that result from the philosophy of the Enlightenment.

Originating in Spanish novels such as the anonymously published *Lazarillo de Tormes* (1554), Mateo Alemán's *Guzmán de*

Alfarache (1599), and Francisco de Quevedo's *El Buscón* (1604), the picaresque novel tells in episodic form the adventures of an antihero on the road. Influenced by Miguel de Cervantes's picaresque novel *Don Quixote* (1605), Henry Fielding's *Joseph Andrews* (1742), *Jonathan Wild* (1743), and *Tom Jones* (1749) are masterful English-language examples of the genre. Exciting adventure stories, these novels employ bawdy humor to present a satiric and panoramic view of eighteenth-century English life.

The picaresque novel as written by Fielding—but also by Tobias Smollett in *Roderick Random* (1748), *Peregrine Pickle* (1750), and *Humphrey Clinker* (1771), and Daniel Defoe in *Moll Flanders* (1722)—gained prominence during the Enlightenment, which emphasized rationality as a means of deriving an authoritative and universal system of ethics and knowledge. The leaders of the Enlightenment saw themselves as shepherding humankind out of the darkness of irrationality and religious superstition and into the light of rationality and science.

The obvious question is why does T. C. Boyle, a young American writer living in late-twentieth-century America, choose to structure his first novel according to the principles of the picaresque? The answer to this question partially comes from Boyle's impatience with the minimalist texts and postmodern meganovels of the 1970s and early 1980s, both of which risk alienating the reader by emphasizing a somber presentation of social issues and/or technical virtuosity at the expense of entertainment and readability. With *Descent of Man*, Boyle had already written a book whose overriding thesis is, as Denis Hennessy has argued, "the unavoidable reversion of humankind to prelapsarian animality, a state of being characterized by physical coarseness and the absence of conscience."[4] In *Water Music*, Boyle constructs a picaresque text that not only entertains the reader but also critiques the rationality, science, and capitalism that characterize the Age of Reason.

Water Music is an entertaining book that observes the two main tenets of popular fiction—it contains memorable characters and an exciting story.[5] One of the main characters, Mungo Park, is a historical eighteenth-century Scottish scientist and explorer who wants to find the source of Africa's Niger River. In a 2000 interview with Mary Heebner, Boyle remembered when he first became interested in Park: "I was doing my Ph.D. in nineteenth-century British literature and was reading John Ruskin, who mentions that Mungo Park was a terrific hero who went to discover the Niger River, but look what he did to his family: he left his wife and kids behind, took off on this adventure and died!"[6] Boyle bases his portrayal of Park on the explorer's own book, *Travels in the Interior Districts of Africa* (1799) and biographies such as T. Banks MacLachlan's *Mungo Park* (1898), Stephen Gwynn's *Mungo Park and the Quest of the Niger* (1934), and Peter Brent's *Black Nile* (1977). *Water Music* follows the general historical trajectory of Park's career from his first, failed expedition from 1795 until 1797 to discover the source of the Niger River to his experiences at his home in Scotland from 1797 until 1805 when he raises his children and writes his book through to his final expedition to Africa during which he loses his life. But, as Boyle told Mary Heebner, he "reinvented Mungo to suit [his] own purposes."[7]

Part of this reinvention is Boyle's exaggeration of the historical material on Park for comic effect. The reader meets Park on the first page of the novel, after the explorer has been taken prisoner by the Moor Ali Ibn Fatoudi, emir of Ludamar, while on his first expedition to find the source of the Niger River in 1795. According to the historical sources, Park was actually imprisoned in such a manner.[8] But the historical sources do not provide the reader with all the comic details that Boyle's exaggerated text provides. Sweltering in his 112-degree tent, Ali examines Park's bare buttocks, comments on their whiteness, and orders Dassoud, his "henchman and human jackal," to hit him with "a lash composed of the caudal appendages of half a dozen wildebeests" (3). The punishment ends when "Mungo's penis, also white, shrank into his body" after the observers crowding the tent's entrance scream "La-la-la-la-la!" in an "excoriating falsetto" that terrifies the explorer (4). Instead of the European man observing the African and classifying him through rational discourse, the African observes and classifies the European man.

This scene and many others in the novel's first section, especially the scene in which the explorer is seduced by and has sex with Ali's overweight wife, Queen Fatima, use dark and absurd humor to characterize Park. In *Travels in the Interior Districts of Africa*, Park describes Queen Fatima as "a woman of the Arab cast, with long black hair, and remarkably corpulent," and she shows him kindness by offering him a bowl of milk.[9] In the seduction and sex scene of *Water Music*, Boyle takes her corpulence and kindness to absurd and comic heights:

> [Park] flings the boots, paws at the buttons, jerks at his *jubbah*. Moist and mountainous, she waits for him, eyes aglow, veil lowered, her flesh smoldering like Vesuvius. He wheezes with haste and anticipation. It's a dream, an attack of fever: no mere mortal could approach this magnificence! He scrambles atop her, feeling for toeholds—so much terrain to explore—mountains, valleys and rifts, new continents, ancient rivers. (58)

Boyle exaggerates the description in Park's text and employs the language of exploration and geographical order to parody the explorer's propriety and essential irrationality.

Ned Rise, Park's alter ego, is a fictional London hustler. Whereas Park is educated, Rise is uneducated and poor. Like Dickensian heroes such as Nicholas Nickleby, David Copperfield, and Pip, Rise wants to escape poverty and rise in the society of his day. But unlike these Dickensian heroes, Rise tries to get ahead in society by breaking the law. A heavy drinker, he not only works as a hustler but as an impresario of live sex shows, a seller of illegal caviar, a grave robber, and, eventually, as a crewman on Park's final African voyage. He even is hanged as a criminal but rises from the dead just as a medical professor is about to dissect his body in an operating theater filled with students.

In addition to creating memorable satiric protagonists in *Water Music*, Boyle constructs an entertaining plot by using metafictional strategies. Boyle himself acknowledged these metafictional strategies in a 1998 interview with Justin D. Coffin: "*Water Music* . . . is pure metafiction."[10] Boyle refers to another text in the title of his first novel: the German-British composer George Frideric Handel's *Water Music*, a three-suite collection of orchestral movements that premiered in the summer of 1717, when the English king George I requested a concert on the Thames River.[11] Like Handel, Boyle intricately structures his text in three parts, simultaneously mocking and paying homage to the composer's equally complex, baroque arrangements. The first part of Boyle's *Water Music*, "The Niger," recounts Park's first African expedition and unsuccessful attempt to find the source of the Niger River from 1795 until 1797 and Rise's initial adventures in the London underworld, which culminate in his arrest, hanging, and apparent death. The second part, "The Yarrow," narrates Park's Scottish sojourn from 1797 until 1805 —his dissatisfaction with his life with his wife, Ailie, and their children, his authorship of *Travels in the Interior Districts of Africa*, and his desire to return to Africa to find the source of the Niger River—as well as Rise's recovery from the botched hanging, adventures as a grave robber, and banishment to Africa, where he joins Park's final expedition. The third part, "Niger Redux," tells of Park's final mad, self-destructive attempt to find the source of the Niger River and of Rise's disapproval of the explorer's scheme. Boyle's coda provides closure to the novel, discussing the fate of Ailie and Rise's newfound success as the messiah of an African tribe that he encounters near the Boussa rapids, where Park and the surviving members of the crew meet their deaths.

Boyle also uses metafiction in two other structural features of *Water Music*. First, Boyle parodies the titles and references the characters of works of fiction that influence the satire and dark comedy of the novel. The section title "Chichikov's Choice" refers to the protagonist of Nikolai Gogol's novel *Dead Souls*, and the section title "All Things That Rise Must Contain Yeast" refers to Flannery O'Connor's last book of short stories, *Everything That Rises Must Converge*. Boyle also parodies popular song titles and refers to their lyrics in his section titles. These references heighten the self-reflexivity and artificiality of Boyle's text. Boyle's comments in a 2005 interview with Robert Birnbaum illuminate the importance of these references: "[In *Water Music*] I am reminding the reader constantly that we are perceiving this through different eyes and through a different culture altogether."[12]

In addition Boyle employs the structural conventions of the nineteenth-century novel in *Water Music* to stress the novel's status as metafiction. In an interview with Elizabeth Adams, Boyle said, "*Water Music* comes out of having done a Ph.D. in nineteenth-century British literature. And reading a hundred three-volume novels from the nineteenth century."[13] Nineteenth-century novels such as George Eliot's *Middlemarch* and Leo Tolstoy's *Anna Karenina* follow two central story lines that allow the reader to compare and evaluate the central characters' ethical decisions and moral actions. These story lines also work together to provide a panoramic overview of society from multiple perspectives. Boyle uses the same structural technique in *Water Music*, braiding the two central story lines of Park and Rise to explore eighteenth-century English society and its ideologies from the explorer's perspective of economic privilege and the hustler's perspective of poverty.

Boyle's language also exaggerates and parodies another convention of the eighteenth- and nineteenth-century novel: melodrama. One of the best examples of Boyle's use of melodrama in the novel is his portrayal of Rise's love affair with Fanny Brunch. In his inflated prose, he describes Fanny's beauty, innocence, and fecundity:

> Fanny Brunch was fresh from the creamery. Her breath was hot with the smell of milk, and it whispered of cribs and nipples and the darkness of the womb. Her skin was cream, her breasts cheeses, there was butter in her smile. When she was fifteen two country louts hacked one another to death over her. With hoes. (124)

Fanny's innocence recalls heroines of Victorian novels. But Boyle's exaggerated language causes the reader to see the absurdity of this virginal fecundity and the response it inspires in men. Unlike her virginal Victorian predecessors, Fanny is more than willing to have sex when the right man arrives. She and Rise have a passionate affair that transforms the hustler's life:

> He woke with Fanny on his mind, hawked fish eggs and thought of nothing else, tumbled into bed with an ache like hunger gnawing at him, swollen and empty at the same time, and dreamed of Fanny, Fanny, Fanny. Women he'd had. Dozens of them. Whores and barmaids, farmgirls, shopgirls, flowergirls, the daughters of fishmongers and tinkers, nurses, nannies, souses and sluts—the Nan Punts and Sally Sebums of the world. A matter of exercising his organ, as simple as that. You put it in, you take it out. But this, this was different. This time his heart was involved. And his mind. (127)

Fanny's beauty, innocence, and other charms have the power to transform Rise from a womanizer into a devoted lover. Boyle conveys the comedy of this transformation by providing an epic list of Rise's previous sexual conquests. The love affair ends when Rise goes to prison and Sir Joseph, her employer, takes an unwilling Fanny to the European continent to live a life of sexual depravity. Like Tess in Thomas Hardy's *Tess of the d'Urbervilles*, Fanny is ruined by a corrupt member of the upper class, but Boyle constructs her melodramatic love affair, ruination at the hands of the evil Sir Joseph, and eventual escape from his clutches as fodder for the reader's laughter.

Water Music includes a final metafictional element in addition to its explicit references to and parodies of the eighteenth- and nineteenth-century novel: superfluous information. The best example is the recipe for stuffed baked camel that Boyle presents in an early passage in which Park attends an African wedding.

After mentioning the ingredients—which include five hundred dates; two hundred plover eggs; twenty two-pound carp; four bustards, cleaned and plucked; two sheep; one large camel; seasonings—and stating that the dish "serves 400" (54), Boyle gives the directions for preparation:

> Dig trench. Reduce inferno to hot coals, three feet in depth. Separately hard-cook eggs. Scale carp and stuff with shelled eggs and dates. Season bustards and stuff with stuffed carp. Stuff stuffed bustards into sheep and stuffed sheep into camel. Singe camel. Then wrap in leaves of doum palm and bury in pit. Bake two days. Serve with rice. (54)

Unnecessary to the advancement of the plot, this information is included for comic effect. Boyle calls attention to the fact that the author of the text can incorporate any and all information that he or she sees fit. By highlighting the writer's role as the fabricator of the text, Boyle illustrates the status of *Water Music* as a random construction.

After deploying his arsenal of postmodern techniques to establish *Water Music* as an homage to and parody of the eighteenth- and nineteenth-century novel in the early sections of the text, Boyle focuses the third section of the novel, "Niger Redux," on delivering a moral pronouncement on Park's explorations and imperialism. Against the advice of his trusted African adviser, Johnson, he plunges ahead with his mission, refusing to turn back and give up on his dream, even when many members of his crew begin dying as a result of accidents. Even when Park faces the Boussa rapids and an army of angry Africans intent on ambushing him, he does not recognize the absurdity of his situation and loses his life and the lives of his crew in the process.

But another character does realize the absurdity of Park's ambition: Johnson, the African-born adviser who lived for many years in England. By having Johnson become the moral center in *Water Music*, Boyle empowers a member of a marginalized race. As Jeff Simon has said in his review of *Water Music*, Johnson, a former American slave who demands a signed edition of the poetry of Alexander Pope in return for his service on Park's second African expedition, recalls Mark Twain's Jim in *The Adventures of Huckleberry Finn* and Cervantes's Sancho Panza in *Don Quixote* as the "wiseguy companion" to the novel's protagonist.[14] Simon's opinion of Johnson applies more to the role the character plays in the first section of *Water Music*, before Park abandons him when he thinks that he has been eaten by a crocodile. In "Niger Redux," on the other hand, Johnson, a reader of Alexander Pope, appears as the voice of reason in the text. Recognizing the danger and futility of Park's obsessive quest, he advises the explorer: "Turn back . . . For me. For your wife and your children" (384). Park's decision not to heed Johnson's advice to avoid using the betrayer Amadi as an adviser leads to his and his crew's demise. A truly rational man, Johnson's moral is that one's life and relationship with one's family are more important and meaningful than the personal renown that comes from making a great discovery.

Boyle also empowers the lower classes in his presentation of Rise's activities at the end of the novel. Like Johnson, Rise is critical of Park's expedition, and while he does not criticize him outright, he battles him for survival. Boyle writes, "The important thing—the bottom—line is still survival. [Rise] hasn't given up his post at the tiller, hasn't stopped battling the explorer for control of his own destiny, though the battle is masked and subtle as it's been from the beginning, from the blistering day he and the blond hero first crossed paths over an open grave at Goree" (421). Rise is concerned with his personal survival, but it is important to remember that Rise and Park come from different social classes, the former from the lower and the latter from the upper. Boyle constructs Rise's secret battle against his dictatorial social superior as class conflict. In surviving the rapids and ambush and becoming the messiah of an African tribe at the end of the novel, Rise distances himself from the rigid social structure of the English class system and is finally "no outcast, no criminal, no orphan" (435). Rise attains the heroism and respect that Park so deeply desires and achieves only in death.

The only Boyle novel not explicitly concerned with America, *Water Music* nevertheless forecasts many of the central concerns of his later novels, all of which are concerned with the conflicting mores, beliefs, and politics of his native land. In the character of Mungo Park, it previews his interest in American history's great dreamers and idealists; in the character of Ned Rise, it demonstrates his affection for America's rebels and outcasts; and in the character of Johnson, it shows his interest in giving voice to the marginalized and oppressed.

Water Music is the work of a postmodern showman who uses parody, metafiction, and wild plots to entertain his reader. But Boyle's first novel is also the work of a serious moralist who has learned from his reading of the minimalists to create heroes from the lower classes and social outcasts. Most important, *Water Music* illustrates Boyle's arrival as a serious and seriously talented American novelist.

Budding Prospects: A Pastoral (1984)

Boyle's second novel, *Budding Prospects*, appeared in 1984.[15] It includes a first-person narrator, a narrative point of view that

Boyle uses in only two other novels: *A Friend of the Earth* and *The Inner Circle*. In addition, at 326 pages *Budding Prospects* is his shortest novel and, much like one of his short stories, features a tight, simple, fast-paced plot that originates in a funny premise. Boyle's hero, a thirty-one-year-old named Felix Nasmyth, and his friends decide to grow and harvest a crop of *Cannabis sativa* in return for half a million dollars in cash. Boyle's text follows Felix and his friends through a series of absurd predicaments and adventures as they work their marijuana farm in the mountains of northern California, near the town of Willits. In an interview Boyle claimed that he found the inspiration for Felix's story in the actual experiences of his friends and pointed out that the novel satirizes the American dream:

> After *Water Music* I was looking for something contemporary. *Budding Prospects* is a story I knew well and was involved in and I just wanted to have some fun with the idea of the quotes—the American dream of getting up early and having a good scam and making your fortune. And in the case of the story as in the fiction, it didn't work. That seems to be a wonderful comment on those ideas and forces you to reevaluate and reassess. As the hero does and as he did in real life.[16]

More than just a simple satire on the American dream, *Budding Prospects* explores the extent to which the values of social equality, freedom of expression, drugs, music, sex, and environmentalism can exist in an America dominated by capitalism. To effect this exploration, Boyle takes the drug use that characterizes part of the hippie ethos and scrutinizes it in the context of the hegemonic capitalist ideology of the 1980s, ultimately deciding that hippie idealism and yuppie capitalism cannot coexist.

The full title of the novel is *Budding Prospects: A Pastoral*, and the subtitle points the reader to Boyle's satire. According to M. H. Abrams, a pastoral is "an elaborately conventional poem expressing an urban poet's nostalgic image of the peace and simplicity of the life of shepherds and other rural folk in an idealized natural setting."[17] Boyle's idealized natural setting is the mountains of northern California, where Felix and his two friends, Gesh and Phil Cherniske, go to farm marijuana for their employer, Vogelsang, and his friend and scientific adviser, Boyd Dowst. Felix describes Vogelsang: "Vogelsang lived in splendid isolation in the hills above Bolinas, making money nefariously, practicing various perversions, collecting power tools, wood carvings, barbers' poles and cases of dry red wine from esoteric little vineyards like Goat's Crouch and Sangre de Cristo" (5). An evil capitalist with a seemingly endless appetite for making and spending money and collecting useless commodities, Vogelsang offers Felix the chance to "make half a million dollars, tax-free" (8). In return for his loot, Vogelsang stipulates, Felix must grow two thousand *Cannabis sativa* plants on a farm in the mountains of northern California. Vogelsang agrees to "put up the capital and provide the land," with Boyd "com[ing] in every few days to oversee the operation" (8). Mesmerized by Vogelsang's voice, which demonically "lift[s] and fall[s] to the pulse" of the popular song "Money (That's What I Want)" (8), Felix accepts the offer, thinking of the enterprise as an easy way to make money: "if Vogelsang was behind it, it would go" (8). By using demonic imagery to characterize Vogelsang and his offer and by clearly indicating that Vogelsang owns the means of production and that Felix is his laborer, Boyle prepares the reader for a satiric critique of capitalism. Boyle effects this critique in a series of scenes in which random natural occurrences and curious interlopers threaten the crop and Vogelsang does not respond to his workers' needs. The stress of laboring in a world determined by nature and the whims of capitalist authority makes a peaceful pastoral existence impossible for Felix and his friends.

Whereas Vogelsang's wealth and materialism clearly distance him from the hippie ethos of social equality, idealism, and munificence, Felix and his friends have a more complicated relationship with the hippie movement. At one point early in the novel, Gesh says, "Society sucks. . . . That happy hippie crap" (29), and Felix agrees with him and elaborates on his point: "The whole hippie ethic—beads, beards, brotherhood, the community of man— it had been bullshit, a subterfuge to keep us from realizing that there were no jobs, the economy was in trouble and the resources of the world going up in smoke. And we'd bought it, lived it, invented it. For all those years" (29). This comment shows Felix's cynical realization of the essential falsity of the hippie ethos, creating a binary relationship between money and hippie idealism. Felix and his friends blame the hippie ethos for the fact that they do not have a lot of money and decide to pursue the accumulation of money at all costs on the marijuana farm. Felix and his friends turn their backs on hippie idealism and embrace the demonic capitalism of Vogelsang.

Boyle satirizes his characters' decision to pursue a capitalist enterprise by creating a seemingly interminable series of threats for them to withstand. Always diminishing the crop's yield and, by extension, their take-home pay, these threats come in three forms: the natural, the mechanical, and the human. Felix's prefatory comments to a passage that discusses a bear that threatens the crop characterize all the natural disasters in the novel, which include rain, rats, and fire: "[The bear] was . . . a manifestation of the wilderness itself, of nature red in tooth and claw, of the teeming, irrational life that surrounds and subsumes us and that our roads and edifices and satellites struggle so hard to deny" (136). In Felix's opinion the stuff of capitalist civilization is no match for the bear, which indicates the ways in which an all-powerful and irrational nature can impinge on and complicate the capitalist attempt to make money. Over the course of a few days, the bear destroys the friends' irrigation system, refuses to eat the poisoned baits that Gesh puts out for it, rummages through their garbage each night, and eventually "in a succession of lightening raids . . . consume[s] three quarts of motor oil, drag[s] a section of barbed-wire fence half a mile into the woods, puncture[s] two more lengths of PVC pipe and knock[s] out the back window of the cabin to get at a case of apricot preserves (which he [eats], shards of glass and all, without apparent harm)" (140). Boyle renders the bear's destructive deeds in a list of epic length, making them appear comic and absurd. In one scene an exasperated Felix and his friends use a gun to hunt the bear, cornering it in a patch of marijuana plants and finding it stoned: "His great chocolate eyes were striated with red veins, marijuana leaves hung from his drooping jaw" (143). When Felix tries to shoot the bear, it escapes, "clear[ing] a path through the scrub that would have accommodated Clyde Beatty's elephants" (144). In this passage the stoned bear demonstrates the extent to which an irrational nature overpowers humanity's rational schemes.

The fire that engulfs the toolshed and destroys part of the crop exemplifies the mechanical disasters that plague Felix and his friends. A drunken Phil starts the fire when he tries to refill a lantern with gas. Felix says, "Drowning in fire, Phil clutched at me. He was dancing—we were dancing—whirling and shouting, frenetic, Laurel and Hardy dropped in a giant's frying pan. My nostrils dilated round the chemical stink of incinerated hair, my flesh touched his and I burned" (242). Besides functioning as a terrific example of Boyle's dark comedy at its absurd best, this passage demonstrates the extent to which a human error can lead to an uncontrollable disaster. The blaze threatens to destroy the shed and the entire crop and to kill Felix and Phil, but after "Gesh emerged from the darkness like all the king's horses and all the king's men" (246), the three friends are able to put it out before it can do too much damage. Felix revels in the "teamwork" of fighting the fire (247), feeling "transcendent, exhilarated, [and] able to leap tall buildings at a single bound" after he and his friends succeed in putting out the fire (250). Boyle satirizes the stupidity of Phil but at the same time praises the friends for their ability to work together as a team.

Humans form the third threat to the success of the crop. The funniest and most absurd of these humans is Officer Jerpbak, a California highway patrolman who menaces Felix throughout the novel. The reader first meets Jerpbak near the beginning of the novel, when Felix bails out Phil from prison. Felix apologizes after accidentally bumping Jerpbak, whose "eyes shone with the fierce fanatical glow of righteousness one recognized in the eyes of Muslim zealots" as he "respond[s] by spinning [Felix] around like an Indian club and slamming [him] back into the wall in the classic shakedown position" (19). In a classic satire of the fascist authoritarian, the fanatical Jerpbak behaves in an extremely violent manner that, being completely out of proportion to the situation, makes the reader laugh. This confrontation between Felix and Jerpbak resembles the confrontations between hippie social protestors and policemen in the 1960s. Throughout the novel Felix worries that Jerpbak will get wind of the operations at the marijuana farm and arrest him; he constantly feels "the threat of Jerpbak" (114). When Felix takes Phil to the hospital after the fire, Boyle condemns Jerpbak's violent authoritarianism when Jerpbak carries an injured boy, whom the text implies he has beaten up, into the emergency room. Felix says, "I backed off as Jerpbak, one arm thrown out for balance, staggered down the hallway under the burden. I'd never seen so much blood. It maculated the floor, darkened the front of Jerpbak's uniform, blotted the features of the limp, spike-haired kid locked under his arm" (255). In this earnest moment, Boyle temporarily abandons the novel's antic comedy to show the disastrous ramifications of authoritarian violence.

In addition to the authoritarian police force, two other people threaten the survival of the marijuana farm: their straitlaced neighbors, Lloyd Sapers and his mentally-challenged son Marlon, who own the property bordering theirs. When Felix, Gesh, and Phil arrive at the farm early in the novel, Vogelsang has already provided a cover for them, telling Lloyd that "he had some friends who were writers—really first-rate, mind you—but that they had a severe and debilitating problem with alcohol. He was going to let them live up at the camp some six or nine months so they could dry out, get some writing done and batten on sunshine and good clean country living" (54–55). The passages in which Felix, Gesh, and Phil try to uphold Vogelsang's ruse are extremely funny, as are the ones in which a paranoid Felix thinks that Lloyd is about to discover that he and his friends are farming marijuana. At one point in the novel, Felix runs into Lloyd at a picnic. When Lloyd tells him that Marlon has found some of their farming equipment, Felix thinks that "the big lumbering half-wit [has] been spying on [them]" and that "Sapers watch[es] [him] like a predator, no hint of amusement in his face" (209–10). Throughout the novel Boyle finds the comedy in the ways in which the paranoid Felix lies to Lloyd as he scrambles to maintain the secret of the marijuana farm.

Boyle uses these natural, mechanical, and human threats to the crop to satirize the American dream. Because of these threats, Felix, Gesh, and Phil experience anxiety and stress despite their hard work, courage, and determination. With each disaster, moreover, they lose more of their crop and take-home pay. As the novel progresses and the disasters of rain, rats, fire, and bear mount, their half million dollars is reduced to fifteen thousand dollars. While the actual laborers see the depletion of their fortune, the capitalist Vogelsang, as Richard Eder reports in his *Los Angles Times* review of the novel, "does very well."[18] By depicting Vogelsang's economic success at the expense of his labor force, Boyle satirizes the ways in which capitalists exploit the working class. But his satire does not stop there. Boyle also indicates the naïveté with which the former hippies accept proposals without examining their possible negative ramifications. Boyle suggests that the hippie ethos does not provide an adequate response to capitalist exploitation. As Felix states early in the novel, the hippie ethos is "bullshit, a subterfuge" that allows for capitalism's continual exploitation of people (29).

Budding Prospects does not end with the bleak conclusion of an exploitative capitalism's victory over hippie idealism. In fact, as Bonnie Lyons has argued, the novel stands apart from many of Boyle's other novels in that it "has a happy ending."[19] This happy ending includes both Felix's confrontation of Vogelsang and his commitment to his relationship with Petra. In the final pages of the novel, Felix travels to Vogelsang's house to question him about the "sad, diminished and tainted gains" of the marijuana crop and his discovery that Vogelsang also has exploited the previous tenant of the farm (312). When Felix arrives at

Vogelsang's house, he sees his former employer sitting among "a pair of skulls, face up, worn the color of weak tea and tessellated like parchment" (315) and other signifiers of death and violence, such as the "guns and knives climbing the walls" (316), "the percussive clank and moribund whine of [a] goatherd's serenade" on his extravagant stereo (316), and his preparations to have sex with the naked Aorta, his girlfriend, and Savoy, who "could almost have been Aorta's twin" (323). These images of death, violence, primitivism, and group sex construct Vogelsang and indicate the ways in which the capitalist descends to a state of animality. After stating that he has lied to them and sold the farmland to the Sapers because Felix and his friends "improved the place for [him]" (321), Vogelsang asks Felix to stay and enjoy his bounty. But Felix decides to leave, rejecting Vogelsang and the exploitative capitalism for which he stands.

In making the moral decision to reject Vogelsang, Felix chooses instead to accept Petra and thereby reaffirms some of the central dictates of hippie idealism. When Felix first meets Petra earlier in the novel, he finds her making pots in her shop and listening to "J. S. Bach sending a glorious full-throated missive to a merciful and present God" (194). Boyle's language is exaggerated in this description, but this does not mean that he wants the reader only to laugh at Felix's reaction to Petra. Petra, who owns her own shop, makes her own pots, and does not purchase useless commodities, firmly opposes Vogelsang's devious exploitation of his laborers and personal unwillingness to work. Petra's "real work" (198), her collection of fifty grotesque dwarves that make Felix laugh, reflects Boyle's own comic and satiric fiction and its grotesque characters. Like Boyle's fiction, Petra's pottery shop exists within the capitalist marketplace, poking fun at it and never exploiting other people. Like Boyle when he writes fiction, Petra is the sole proprietor of her enterprise. In rejecting Vogelsang for Petra, Felix accepts the hippie ideals of artistic creation, self-sufficiency, sex, and procreation. As Felix drives away from Vogelsang's house at the end of the novel, he thinks of Petra's "hands, sunk in the raw clay, kneading it like bread, molding it, pulling it hard, lasting stuff from its shifting, shapeless core. Wet, yielding, fecund" (325). This image of artistic creation combines with the image of sexual creation in the novel's last words—Felix looks forward to the "long rainy winter ahead of [him], time to think things over, break some new ground, and maybe even—if things went well—to plant a little seed" (326)— to suggest the possibility of Felix creating a truly pastoral life with Petra.

Budding Prospects demonstrates the ways in which a man overcomes his cynicism to embrace, perhaps for the first time, the dictates of hippie idealism. Using Felix's final decision, Boyle sets Petra's artistic creativity, sexuality, self-sufficiency, and rejection of Jerpbak's authoritarianism against the exploitative capitalism of Vogelsang, which he presents as destructive and barbaric. *Budding Prospects* is a hilarious and earnest reminder that America in the 1980s is in dire need of some 1960s idealism.

World's End (1987)

Critics generally regard *World's End*, Boyle's third novel and winner of the PEN/Faulkner Award for fiction in 1988, as his first major novel.[20] Like *Water Music* and *Budding Prospects*, *World's End* is a very funny novel, but its comedy is darker. In addition *World's End* is more structurally and thematically ambitious than Boyle's previous two novels, telling a multigenerational story of three families—the Van Brunts, the Van Warts, and the Mohonks—that transpires in the Hudson Valley of New

York in the seventeenth and twentieth centuries. In both centuries class and race divide the three families, starting in the seventeenth century, when the wealthy Van Warts own the land that the Van Brunts farm as their tenants, and the Mohonks, a family from the tribe of Kitchawank Indians, suffer the ramifications of being forcibly displaced from their land. The action of the novel centers on the class and racial strife that this situation creates among the families. Most of the action takes place in Peterskill, New York, a fictional town that Boyle loosely bases on his hometown of Peekskill and creates under the influence of Gabriel García Márquez's Macondo, the setting of the novel *One Hundred Years of Solitude* and other works of his fiction, and William Faulkner's Yoknapatawpha County. Boyle's debt to García Márquez, whom he called "the best writer alive" in an interview with Elizabeth Adams,[21] also appears in his use of magical realism, as well as in the novel's structure as a multigenerational family saga. The reliance of *World's End* on the texts of García Márquez and Boyle's strategy of drawing parallels between the activities of the families in the seventeenth and twentieth centuries give the novel a more finely wrought structure than *Water Music* and *Budding Prospects*. But even though *World's End* is structurally different from the two previous novels, it continues Boyle's exploration of class and race differences.

As Boyle's most autobiographical novel, *World's End* departs significantly from *Water Music* and *Budding Prospects*. Boyle acknowledged the novel's autobiographical nature in his 1998 interview with Justin D. Coffin: "One genius critic said that *World's End* is a kind of fictional autobiography. And I loved that, because that's what it is. I don't know my genealogy much: I would just rather invent it."[22] Boyle's starting point for the fictional autobiography and genealogy in *World's End* is his creation of his chief protagonist, Walter Van Brunt, and his primary setting of Peterskill, New York. Like Boyle, Walter was born in the late 1940s and is in his early twenties in the late 1960s. The hippie subculture of drugs, sex, and music attracts Walter, much as it did the young Boyle, not because of his philosophical beliefs, but because he enjoys the freedom of the scene. As Boyle said in his 2003 interview with C. P. Farley, he "kind of drift[ed] into the scene for its own sake without having much deep philosophy involved in it."[23] The first section of *World's End* indicates that Walter shares the young Boyle's approach to hippie practices. He spends the night of his birthday getting drunk and doing drugs with his friends Hector and Benny and having sex with Mardi Van Wart, a girl he meets that night. Boyle refers to Walter's enthusiasm for existentialist and nihilistic literature and philosophy to suggest the extent to which he does not believe in the hippie ideals of love, peace, and social consciousness: "It was 1968. Sartre was front-page news, the *Saturday Review* was asking 'Can We Survive Nihilism?' and *Life* had photographed Jack Gelber adrift on an ice floe. Walter knew all about it. He was an alienated hero himself, he was a Meursault, a Rocquentin, a man of iron and tears facing the world in unhope and as riddled with nausea as a Jarlsberg is with holes" (6). Walter constructs himself as a nihilist who opposes the hippie philosophy, but the reader laughs at his immature posturing. In creating the autobiographical Walter as a comical nihilist, Boyle both gains emotional detachment from his own past and invites the reader to laugh at the disaffected young man he himself once was.

Walter's relationship with his parents constitutes another autobiographical element in the text. In his 1990 interview with and profile of Boyle, Tad Friend noted that "Boyle's own innocence died young in Peekskill, N.Y. His father, a school-bus driver, and his mother, a secretary, were alcoholics."[24] While Boyle's parents, as autobiographical stories such as "If the River Was Whiskey" make clear, were emotionally absent when he was growing up, Walter's parents are physically absent. Truman, Walter's father, abandons his family after he betrays his wife and friends in an anti-Communist riot in Peterskill in 1949 when Walter was still a toddler. Shortly after Truman's flight, Christina, Walter's mother, starves herself to death as a result of her grief and gives her son to her friends Lola and Hesh Solovay to raise. As did Boyle himself, Walter grows up without the attention of his parents and subsequently struggles to find meaning in life.

Boyle's construction of Peterskill as a fictional version of his native Peekskill also connects *World's End* to his life. Like the fictional Peterskill, Peekskill is located in the Hudson River Valley of New York near West Point and was established in the seventeenth century when Dutch traders began exchanging manufactured goods with the resident population, a tribe of Indians known as the Sackhoes from the Kitchawank sachemdom.[25] In addition, according to historian Michael Kammen, the anti-Communist riot of 1949, in which many of the central characters in the novel participate, happened in Peterskill.[26] As reviewer Michiko Kakutani argues, Boyle in *World's End* explores this historical material "to tackle the complicated issues of freedom, class and race involved in the founding of our nation."[27]

Boyle employs the quest for the father as his point of departure for his analysis of freedom, class, and race in American history. Walter goes on a quest to find his father, Truman. The quest begins in 1968, when the drunk and high Walter and Mardi go skinny-dipping on the night of his birthday and swim out to the defunct World War II ships "that lay anchored in thirty feet of water off Dunderberg Mountain" (11). While aboard one of the ships, Walter is accosted by a vision of many ghosts, including that of his grandmother and still-living but missing father—Boyle here obviously nods to Hamlet's catalytic conversation with his father's ghost at the beginning of Shakespeare's play. Upon seeing the visions, Walter wants to ask his father why he abandoned his family and betrayed his Communist friends and wife during the riot of 1949: "There was unfinished business here, something he had to ask, had to know" (16). This passage, which shows Boyle's debt to both the magical realism of García Márquez's *One Hundred Years of Solitude* and the fantastic tales of Washington Irving, represents the beginning of Walter's quest. When later that night Walter crashes his motorcycle near a historical marker commemorating the seventeenth-century execution of Cadwallader Crane and Jeremy Mohonk, two friends who elsewhere in the novel rebel against the authority of the patroon Oloffe Stephanus Van Wart and are subsequently betrayed and turned in by Walter's ancestor and namesake, Wouter Van Brunt, he literally collides with history, losing his right foot in the process. At this point early in the novel, Walter does not know that Wouter is a traitor, but Boyle's darkly comic depiction of his accident indicates that he cannot escape this knowledge. *World's End*, accordingly, tells the story of Walter's quest to discover, through his eventual meeting with Truman and reading of his father's manuscript on the history of Van Brunt–Van Wart–Mohonk relations later in the novel, that betrayal is the central theme that underlies his family's history. The question is whether Walter can escape the traitorous fate of Wouter and Truman.

Walter has every opportunity to escape this fate. At the beginning of the novel, the ghost of Piet, a modern-day oracle in the tradition of the admonitory Greek prophet Tiresias and Truman's coconspirator in the betrayal of the Communists, warns him: "Now don't you go following in your father's footsteps, hear?" (16). Despite two motorcycle accidents that deprive him of both his feet, Walter makes a series of decisions that align him with Truman as a traitor, including his betrayal of his wife, Jessica, when he has an adulterous affair with Mardi; his rape of Jessica; his friendship with and acceptance of a job working for Mardi's father, Depeyster, at Depeyster Manufacturing; and his attempt to sabotage his friend Tom Crane's environmentalist research and teaching boat, *Arcadia*. All of these decisions draw Walter away from the politics and philosophies of his adoptive parents, Lola and Hesh Solovay, who are victims in the riot of 1949, and of the hippies Jessica and Tom, and they bring him closer to the racism and superficiality of the Van Warts.

Boyle's satiric depiction of the Van Warts makes *World's End* one of his most politically engaged novels. The main villain of the novel's sections on the 1960s, Depeyster Van Wart, is a despicable character, a racist who hates Walter's adoptive parents because they are "Jews, Communists, the worst" (157). Throughout the novel Depeyster attempts to impregnate his alienated wife, Joanna, and produce a male heir to his estate, Van Wart Manor, and to extend his land holdings to include the property of Peletiah Crane and his hippie son, Tom, taking great joy when the former suffers a fatal stroke. In addition Depeyster plays a crucial role in the riot of 1949, leading the conservative rabble who mercilessly beat the Communists and working people who have gathered to attend a picnic and a concert. The reader meets Depeyster at the beginning of the "Ancestral Dirt" chapter:

> Depeyster Van Wart, twelfth heir to Van Wart Manor,
> the late seventeenth-century house that lay just outside
> Peterskill on Van Wart Ridge where it commanded a sweep-
> ing view of the town dump and the rushing, refuse-clogged
> waters of Van Wart Creek, was a terraphage. That is, he ate
> dirt. . . . ancestral dirt, scooped with a garden digger from
> the cool weatherless caverns beneath the house. (33)

This passage begins with Boyle's formal description of the equally
formal land holdings of the Van Wart family, but its tone quickly
becomes absurd and comic when it characterizes Depeyster as a
terraphage. In making this quick tonal shift, Boyle creates a weird
image to ensure that his reader remembers Depeyster as a deca-
dent and wealthy landowner who literally ingests and is addicted
to the dirt that constitutes his dead ancestral past.

Throughout *World's End*, Depeyster tempts Walter away
from his politically radical heritage. Raised by the Communists
Hesh and Lola, married for a while to the environmentalist Jessica, and friends with Tom Crane, Walter is surrounded by politically radical and progressive characters. In the sections of the
novel on the riot of 1949, the peaceful Hesh and Lola work with
Walter's parents to organize the concert. In the sections of
the novel on the late 1960s, Jessica and Tom live their hippie
ideals by holding jobs that promote environmentalism. Tom, the
novel's "Saint of the Forest," even resides for a while Thoreau-
like in the woods, in a secluded cabin without heat and electric-
ity. Eventually Depeyster offers a job to Walter. After accepting
the job, Walter abandons his hippie dress and hair, becomes
Depeyster's protégé, and is so friendly with his employer that he
calls him "Dipe." As the novel progresses, Depeyster functions
more and more as a father figure for Walter, exposing him to
his ideology and attempting to convince him that Truman is a

patriot for betraying the concertgoers in 1949: "Your father," he tells Walter early in the novel, "your father was a patriot" (124). As a nihilist and depressed over the loss of his feet, Walter is especially vulnerable to Depeyster's discourse, which involves him deeply with his boss at the expense of his relationships with his friends.

Boyle also uses his satiric method to characterize Depeyster's daughter, Mardi, as a superficial hippie and Walter's temptress. Unlike Jessica and Tom, Mardi dresses like a hippie and indulges in drug use and free love without basing her actions on deeply held philosophical beliefs, such as equal social rights for members of all racial groups. She demonstrates her nihilism in her affair with Walter and her reliance on her father's wealth to finance her lifestyle. Walter, in turn, reaffirms his nihilism by choosing to have a fleeting affair with Mardi rather than a stable marriage to Jessica, thereby aligning himself with the exploitative Van Wart clan.

Depeyster and Mardi's actions in the late 1960s originate in their ancestors' actions in the seventeenth century. In this context, Michael Kammen has discussed the sense of fatalism that underlies the novel,[28] and Boyle himself, in his essay "History on Two Wheels," has acknowledged the extent to which "genetic determinism" in the text dooms his characters to repeat history.[29] According to Boyle the decisions of past family members determine the decisions of family members in the present and, accordingly, the course of history. This determinism, which recalls the literary naturalism of authors such as Jack London, a writer to whom the characters of *World's End* repeatedly refer, most obviously connects Wouter, Truman, and Walter Van Brunt as traitors who ensure the victory and survival of rich and powerful families such as the Van Warts over people of laboring classes and marginalized races. But this determinism also demonstrates the ways in which powerful figures such as Stephanus Van Wart, the son of the first patroon, exploit laborers and marginalized races and how this exploitation continues in the twentieth-century actions of Depeyster. A major uprising against the authority of the Van Warts occurs when Wouter Van Brunt disagrees with Stephanus Van Wart's seemingly arbitrary decision to terminate his lease and, with the help of Cadwallader Crane and Jeremy Mohonk, starts a riot in which some Van Wart property is destroyed. Even though Wouter is the major instigator of the riot, he turns in Cadwallader and Jeremy, whom Stephanus executes to demonstrate his power. Stephanus's exploitation of his laborers and his decision to execute the rebels for a minor offense in the seventeenth century determine Depeyster's attempt to consolidate his power in the twentieth century by leading the violent attack on the peaceful concertgoers in 1949, attempting to produce a male heir, and trying to take over the Crane property. Depeyster's actions illustrate Karl Marx's famous dictum "History repeats itself, first as tragedy, second as farce," with the riot of 1949 as the tragic repetition of the executions of Cadwallader and Jeremy and the attempt to produce the male heir and extend the property as its farcical repetition.

In pointing out the "genetic determinism" of history, Boyle in *World's End* appears to reach the extremely pessimistic conclusion that all revolutionary action against the hegemony of powerful people, such as the Van Warts, is ultimately futile. Unlike in *Budding Prospects*, where Felix disavows his inherent cynicism and embraces hippie idealism through his relationship with Petra, Boyle in *World's End* seems to view hippie idealism as both an outgrowth of capitalism and as an ineffective response

to it. But if this view were the only case, Boyle would not emphasize the theme of betrayal so thoroughly. The three major traitors in the Van Brunt family—Wouter, Truman, and Walter—all
have the opportunity to reject the ideologies of the Van Warts
and accept the progressive ideologies of Jessica and the Solovay
and Crane families. Boyle's emphasis on the irreducible relationship between individual decisions and historical events relates to
the way in which he highlights existentialism in his characterization of Walter. Walter is very aware of the nihilistic aspect of the
philosophies of Sartre and Camus but is unaware of how these
philosophies argue for the creation of just societies through the
decisions and actions of individuals. While showing the tragic
and eventually farcical decisions and actions of the Van Brunt
traitors, Boyle in *World's End* offers the reader the possibility of
choosing progressive courses of action that reject the dictates of
the establishment exemplified by the Van Warts.

The Solovay and Crane families and Jessica represent the radical, progressive, and hippie philosophies to which the Van Warts
and the Van Brunts, through the traitorous decisions and actions
of Wouter, Truman, and Walter, are opposed. As Communists
and activists for the rights of the working class and racial equality, Hesh and Lola Solovay, along with radical activists Sasha
Freeman and Morton Blum, play a prominent role in organizing
the concert of 1949, for which they schedule Paul Robeson to
sing. The chapter titled "Patrimony" narrates how the concert
organizers assume that the event "was going to be a peaceful affair, Negroes and whites together, working people, women and
children and old folks, enjoying a concert and maybe a couple of
political speeches, exercising their rights to assemble and to
express unpopular ideas" (86). Truman's abandonment of his

friends and his decision to inform on them to the "anti-Communist, anti-Jew and anti-Negro" contingent led in part by Depeyster Van Wart propagates a racially motivated tragedy in which members of Depeyster's rabble yell insults, including "Nigger lovers," "Kikes," and "Commie Jew bastards" (87), destroy property, and mercilessly beat peaceful concertgoers.

While the Solovays signify the radical politics of the late 1940s and early 1950s, the Cranes, and in particular Tom Crane, signify the hippie ethos of the late 1960s. Tom's two most important ancestors in the novel, Cadwallader and his grandfather Peletiah, share his love of nature, perhaps making him genetically predisposed to have affection for the environment. Tom, unlike the superficial Mardi and the self-avowed nihilist Walter, authentically lives his hippie philosophy. Boyle's presentation of the naive Tom at times borders on caricature—as when he comically describes the *Arcadia* from Tom's perspective as "a floating shack christened in and dedicated to all the great hippie ideals—to long hair and vegetarianism, astrology, the snail darter, Peace Now, satori, folk music and goat turd mulching" (426)—but he admires him for his earnestness and enthusiasm, two characteristics that are in sharp contrast to those of the Van Warts and Van Brunts and that align him with Cadwallader and Peletiah. The best example of Tom's earnestness and enthusiasm occurs after he gets a job on the *Arcadia*. Boyle discusses Tom's feelings for the boat: "Tom Crane loved her. Loved her unreservedly. Loved her right down to the burnished cleats on the caprail and the discolored frying pans that hung above the woodstove in the galley" (425). With the passage continuing on to describe more parts of the boat in detailed prose, Boyle conveys Tom's earnest passion for his workplace. Tom's job on the boat, which stops at ports on the Hudson River and whose crew teaches people about aquatic life and conservation, provides an important connection with Hesh and Lola. Like the Solovays before him, Tom engages in a political struggle against conservatism—Depeyster and his friends oppose the boat, just as they opposed the concert in 1949—with enthusiasm and earnestness. Tom even uses the money that Depeyster pays him for his property at the end of the novel to repair the *Arcadia* after Walter damages it in an attempt to destroy it.

By the end of the novel, Jessica has begun a relationship with Tom that contrasts sharply with her earlier relationship with Walter. Instead of staying at home to provide for Walter and endure the disgrace of his affair with Mardi, Jessica shows her independence in her relationship with Tom by deciding to study marine biology at New York University. Jessica and Tom move into his deceased grandfather's house with "its gleaming appurtenances of modernity, with its dishwasher, its toaster, its TV, its paved driveway and carpeted halls" (426), but they still pursue their hippie ideals by attending graduate school and working on the *Arcadia*. Like Felix and Petra in *Budding Prospects*, Jessica and Tom form a small contingent of progressive individuals in which hippie idealism survives.

The Mohonk family, in turn, complicates Boyle's belief that the individual can choose between progressive and conservative political beliefs. The four major young characters in the novel's sections on the late 1960s—Walter, Mardi, Jessica, and Tom— are friends with people from other races, including the Hispanic Hector and an African American lover of Mardi's, but they, for the most part, seem unaware of the persistent problem of racial inequality in America. Boyle includes the sections on the Mohonk family to consider the relationship between progressive political ideals and the pursuit of racial equality.

As the sections of *World's End* set in the seventeenth century make clear, the inhabitation of America by white European settlers is based on a system of racial and social injustice. Under this system the Van Brunt family obtained passage from Holland to the Hudson Valley and "a five-morgen farm a mile or so beyond Jan Pieterse's trading post at the mouth of Acquasinnick Creek, on land that had lately been the tribal legacy of the Kitchawanks" in return for their agreement to be "indentured servants to the Van Warts for all their days on earth" (19). As powerful land owners the Van Warts exploit the Van Brunts, accruing money and goods from them, and take away the land of the Kitchawanks, whom they consider inferior and savage. Here Boyle points out that America is founded on social and racial inequalities that are created in the interests of capitalism.

Despite the class and racial differences that separate the Van Warts, Van Brunts, and Mohonks, the three families are connected in a more complex system of power relations than economic class. Mohonk, a member of the Kitchawank tribe and founder of the Mohonk family, and Katrinchee Van Brunt have a child, Jeremy Mohonk, who eventually participates in the rebellion against the patroon Stephanus Van Wart. Mohonk's interracial relationship with Katrinchee complicates the capitalist system that uses race to define economic class. Jeremy Mohonk, the offspring of that relationship, is of mixed race, a cultural hybrid who, when he chooses to leave the Dutch settlement and live as a Kitchawank, reveals the arbitrary nature of racial classifications. Boyle's references to interracial relationships and the construction of race identity indicate the complicated power dynamics that exist within the Van Wart–Van Brunt–Mohonk matrix, which, for Boyle, is a microcosm of the social structure on which America is founded.

The second Jeremy Mohonk, the last surviving member of the Kitchawank tribe, experiences the ramifications of this social structure in the twentieth century. Jeremy exemplifies the racial hybridity that demonstrates the essential falsity of racial classifications. Despite his mixed-race heritage, Jeremy, like his namesake and ancestor before him, lives as and takes pride in being a Kitchawank. Because he was born on a reservation, this racial identity is forced on him, but he ultimately chooses to take pride in his heritage. Jeremy meets and falls under the influence of the novelist, Marxist, and future co-organizer of the 1949 concert, Sasha Freeman, who writes a book entitled *Marx among the Mohicans* and instructs Jeremy to read "Marx, Lenin and Trotsky, Bakunin, Kropotkin, Proudhon, Fourier" to teach him that "property is theft, that destruction is a kind of creation, that the insurrectionary deed is the most efficacious means of propaganda" (185).

Like Depeyster, the radicalized Jeremy wants to have a child to continue his line, and he has the affair with Joanna with this intention in mind: "He wanted . . . a son who had less of the Kitchawank in him and more of the people of the wolf. This son would be no blessing, no purveyor of grace or redemption. This son would be his revenge" (357). Writing about Depeyster's reaction to the birth of "his" son, Boyle concludes the novel: "There it was—there *he* was—his son, swaddled in white linen like the others, but big, too big, and with a brushstroke of tarry black hair on his head. And there was something wrong with his skin too—he was dark, coppery almost, as if he'd been sunburned or something" (455). Even as Depeyster's decision to accept the baby as his own and name him "Rombout" suggests the continued propagation of his power in the face of Jeremy's action and, as Theo D'haen has argued, "confirms and even rigidifies the status quo,"[30] it also indicates the extent to which his power deludes him. Regardless of Depeyster's decision, Jeremy successfully infiltrates the Van Wart family, creating in the baby the racial hybridity that may one day inspire him to reject Depeyster and choose the racial identity of the Kitchawank.

At the conclusion of *World's End*, Boyle reconciles the way of the wolf—that is, the way of sneakiness and dishonesty—with the hippie ideals of Tom and Jessica as a means of rebelling against the establishment. As earnest hippies, Tom and Jessica make some concessions to capitalism and the establishment, but in so doing, they continue to fight for their environmentalist beliefs from within the system. Depeyster Van Wart, on the other hand, attempts to hide the mixed-race origin of his son and continues to extend his intolerant racial beliefs and his economic power over the people of Peterskill. Boyle holds out hope that Jeremy Mohonk can appropriate the sneaky ways of Depeyster and use them, in the hybridity of the young Rombout Van Wart, to rebel against Depeyster's hegemony. At the end of *World's End*, Boyle leaves his reader with two reconciled means of rebellion against authority: the crafty and cynical way of Jeremy and the earnest way of Tom and Jessica. As a novel that denounces authoritarianism from within the system of capitalism and presents hippie idealism as a possible response to racism, classicism, and other forms of social injustice, *World's End* exemplifies both means of rebellion.

Unlike Jeremy Mohonk, Tom, and Jessica, Walter Van Brunt decides not to rebel against Depeyster's authoritarian establishment but conforms to it. Even though he claims to be an existentialist, he only superficially understands the nihilism of Sartre and Camus as a philosophy that posits the meaninglessness of existence. He never recognizes that this nihilism allows human-ity the freedom to be responsible to other people and create a socially just society. When this superficial existentialist completes his quest for the father and visits Truman at his home in Barrow, Alaska, the northernmost city in the United States, and reads Truman's long history of racial and class conflict in Peterskill, he discovers the traitorous nature of the Van Brunt family. The deci-sion to betray one's friends and progressive ideals, for Boyle, defines historical irresponsibility and results in the emotional coldness of both Truman and Walter. Just as Truman lives in the coldest city in the United States, Walter freezes to death after his jealousy leads him to attempt to sabotage the *Arcadia*. For the existentialists Sartre and Camus and the characters Jeremy, Jes-sica, and Tom, the passionate decision to rebel against authori-tarianism is a blow against emotional detachment from other people and the tragedy of a cyclical history that results in the continued marginalized existence of minorities and the poor.

CHAPTER 4

T. C. Boyle's Novels of the 1990s
East Is East, The Road to Wellville,
The Tortilla Curtain, and *Riven Rock*

In a 2003 interview with Robert Birnbaum, T. C. Boyle acknowledged the tendency of his books to build on themes that he addressed in previous books,[1] and his novels of the 1990s are no exception to this tendency. Two of them, *East Is East* and *The Tortilla Curtain*, take up the issue of racism, which Boyle originally considered in *Water Music* and *World's End*, and explore it in the context of illegal immigration. In so doing, Boyle places *East Is East* and *The Tortilla Curtain* in the tradition of socially engaged novels, a genre to which he in a 2000 interview with Judith Handschuh acknowledged his debt: "I do seem to be more interested in social and historical matters than many American writers of our time, and I look to writers like Dickens and Mark Twain, not to mention Steinbeck and Dos Passos, for inspiration."[2] If *East Is East* gives Dickens and Twain a postmodern spin in its satire of American racism, then *The Tortilla Curtain* provides a more somber discussion of the relationship between poverty and class that intentionally recalls *The Grapes of Wrath*.

Boyle also published two other novels, *The Road to Wellville* and *Riven Rock*, in the 1990s, both of which pick up the thematic consideration of the relationship among idealism, science, and authoritarianism found in *Water Music* and apply it to specific American movements that were prominent during the early years of the twentieth century: the health-food and exercise craze, which Dr. John Harvey Kellogg's sanitarium at Battle Creek, Michigan, exemplifies in *The Road to Wellville*, and the interest in psychiatry and feminism that is found in *Riven Rock*. Like *Water Music*, both *The Road to Wellville* and *Riven Rock* are historical novels that include fictional and real-life characters. Dr. John Harvey Kellogg in *The Road to Wellville* and the psychiatrists in *Riven Rock* are historical figures that Boyle uses to consider the ways in which science and idealistic beliefs combine to form messianic messages that result in megalomania and authoritarianism. He also uses these figures to explore what happens when people fall under their influence and surrender their freedom in the process. For Boyle this process of surrendering freedom is typically American and results in disaster and unhappiness. In *The Road to Wellville*, Boyle discusses his themes of idealism, authoritarianism, and submission in a comic style that recalls *Water Music* and *Budding Prospects*, whereas in *Riven Rock* his darker comedy and more somber tone align that novel with *World's End* and *The Tortilla Curtain*.

East Is East (1990)

"Boyle's fourth novel, *East Is East* (1990)," writes Bonnie Lyons, "was inspired by a newspaper article from a friend who dropped by while Boyle was writing *World's End* and announced he had found Boyle a subject for his next book."[3] As Lyons relates, this subject is "Hiro (hero) Tanaka, a twenty-year-old Japanese seaman [who] jumps ship off the Georgia coast, swims ashore, and tries to survive as an illegal alien."[4] Boyle tells Hiro's story to explore racism, an issue that he first considered in the historical context of eighteenth-century imperialism in *Water Music*, then both in the seventeenth-century colonialism and the radical and progressive politics of the McCarthy era and the late 1960s in *World's End*. The contemporary setting of *East Is East*—Georgia in the year 1990—allows Boyle to explore current American attitudes on race.[5] Boyle told Elizabeth Adams in an interview that "[*East Is East*] concerns some of the themes of *Water Music*: racism in particular, cultural predetermination, cultural dislocation."[6] The characters of *East Is East*, most of whom are Immigration and Naturalization Service (INS) officials, local police officers, and writers living in the Thanatopsis House writers' colony on Tupelo Island, demonstrate these attitudes in their interactions with Hiro, which illustrate their stance on the issue of illegal immigration. Throughout the novel Boyle contrasts the intense physical sufferings of Hiro, which primarily transpire in the swamps of Georgia, to the petty sufferings of the writers working in the cushy environment of Thanatopsis House. One of these writers is Ruth Dershowitz, the novel's other chief character. Ruth, a mildly talented writer, initially befriends and helps Hiro, but she eventually chooses to advance her career rather than continue to offer him her assistance. Like Walter Van Brunt in *World's End*, Ruth is a traitor in her betrayal of Hiro.

East Is East opens at night, when Hiro jumps from his ship *Tokachi-maru*, swims toward the Georgia coast, climbs onto a moored boat, and encounters Ruth in the act of making love to her boyfriend, Saxby Lights, the wealthy son of Septima, the owner of Thanatopsis House. A lack of cultural awareness defines Hiro's initial perceptions of America. He initially sees America as an alternative to the racism that he experiences in his native country: "Americans, he knew, were a polyglot tribe, mutts and mulattoes and worse—or better, depending on your point of view. In America you could be one part Negro, two parts Serbo-Croatian and three parts Eskimo and walk down the street with your head held high" (17). When Hiro begins to experience American racism later in the novel, however, he quickly realizes the falsity of his original view of America, which he constructed based on the myth of America as melting pot, as well as on his exposure to American popular culture. Like Walter Van Brunt in *World's End*, Hiro embarks on a quest to find his father, only for him this quest is embedded in American popular culture, many of the key elements of which signify the attainment of freedom.

When Hiro jumps off the *Tokachi-maru*, he takes with him a copy of *The Way of the Samurai*, in which Japanese novelist Yukio Mishima interprets for the twentieth century Jōchō Yamamoto's *Hagakure* (or samurai) code. This code includes such *bushido* virtues as rectitude, courage, benevolence, respect, honesty, honor, and loyalty.[7] Boyle remarks on Hiro's relationship to *The Way of the Samurai*: "He'd read deeply in *The Way of the Samurai* for days, getting Mishima's and Jōchō's words by heart, and now he was ready. The book—in its plastic womb and with the odd little green bills and his father's picture nestled safely between its leaves—clung to him with tentacles of black electrician's tape" (19). By reading *The Way of the Samurai*, Hiro learns about "glory" (94), that "society . . . was corrupt, emasculated, obsessed with material things, with the pettiness of getting and taking, selling and buying" (94), and a way to "conquer [his feeling of inferiority]" (95). With Mishima's book strapped to his body, Hiro is a walking text, a hero (or Hiro) whose reading constructs his identity.

Throughout the novel Boyle juxtaposes comic scenes—in his 2000 interview with Judith Handschuh, Boyle said that he "consider[s] *East Is East* a very funny book"[8]—and serious scenes to create a sense of uneasiness in readers, making them realize that they are laughing at serious matters. These tonal shifts stress the ways in which racism is institutionalized in the American government. Heather J. Hicks notes that Detlef Abercorn, an INS official in the novel, is "afflicted by vitiligo, a condition that leaves him spotted with whiteness" and that this condition marks "the presence of a white supremacist sensibility within the activities of [the INS]."[9] Detlef thinks of Hiro as "the AWOL Nip on Tupelo Island" (54), and his partner Lewis Turco "fum[es] over this crazed, inconsiderate, raging pain in the ass of a Japanese Nip—he hated the son of a bitch already, hoped they tarred and feathered him and sent him home to Nagasaki or whatever in a box" (57). Detlef's and Lewis's racist attitudes are influenced by their perceptions of Hiro, which are formulated in response to his classification as an "IAADA—Illegal Alien, Armed, Dangerous and Amok" (53), as well as an official report that he committed "UNPROVOKED ATTACKS ON EYEWITNESSES LIGHTS SAXBY DERSHOWITZ RUTH WHITE OLMSTEAD FIRST DEGREE BURNS ARSON FIRE TOTAL LOSS" (55). Hiro's so-called crimes result from racial intolerance and his inability to communicate with the Americans whom he encounters, not from any intent on his part to harm people. Boyle suggests that the American government is not equipped to evaluate the intentions of so-called criminals and therefore cannot arrive at the truth of criminal actions. Like the classificatory discourse in *Water Music*, the government's language in *East Is East* is false, pernicious, and propagates racial stereotypes.

At the outset of *East Is East* and roughly throughout its first half, Boyle presents Ruth Dershowitz as a possible friend and ally of Hiro's, one who rejects the racist attitudes of the INS officials and her boyfriend Saxby Lights. When Hiro first alights on

Saxby's boat, Ruth shows compassion and concern for him by asking Saxby to rescue him from drowning. Later in the novel Ruth notices that Hiro is living in the woods surrounding Thanatopsis House and leaves food out for him. Eventually she decides to hide him in her room, away from both the residents of Thanatopsis House and the INS officials.

Ruth's attitude toward Hiro changes when she begins to perceive him not as an individual but as a pawn in the game of her personal life. Ruth, therefore, functions as both Hiro's friend and nemesis in the novel. She shows her friendship for Hiro when she initially helps him, but she begins to serve as his nemesis when she involves him in her personal life. Inspired by Hiro, Ruth begins writing a Japanese story entitled "Of Tears and the Tide" (118), but this story, unlike Boyle's novel *East Is East*, is not written by a socially engaged writer interested in racism and illegal immigration. The author of "Of Tears and the Tide" is more interested in advancing her career as a writer. Boyle demonstrates Ruth's careerist interest by the way in which she fixates on the successful but superficial writer Jane Shine. Writing from Ruth's perspective in the "Rusu" chapter, Boyle indicates how she compares her limited success as a writer to Jane's greater success: "Jane's stories appeared in *Esquire*, *The New Yorker* and the *Partisan Review*, and then she had a collection out and her picture was everywhere and the critics—the exclusively male critics—fell over dead with the highest, most exquisite praise of their careers on their dying lips" (121). Despite Ruth's correct assessment that Jane uses her image and sexuality to advance her career at the expense of the quality of her writing, Ruth wastes many hours dwelling on Jane's popularity—she stays up one night with "her mind pounding on like a machine out of control: *God, how she loathed that bitch!*" (127)—rather than the quality of her own writing. Ruth's obsession with Jane and her own lack of success as a writer become more pronounced later in the novel, when she gives a reading for the residents of Thanatopsis House. The reading is a disaster, putting the more elderly residents to sleep—"Orlando Sneezers began to snore" and "Septima was nodding in her chair" (331)—and prompting Jane to "rise from the couch to stretch and yawn theatrically, yawing the mass of her hair this way and that and exchanging some nasty little witticism with Mignonette Teitelbaum and the gaping, blinking, eye-rubbing, nose-blowing form of Orlando Sneezers" (332). Ruth's boring, decidedly un-Boyle-like reading indicates that her career and obsession with Jane are more important to her than her relationship with Hiro and her initial rejection of racism. Indeed, before Ruth gives her reading, she tells Saxby, "All I want to see is Hiro Tanaka in jail and this whole ordeal over with" (330).

Boyle contrasts Ruth's disastrous reading with Hiro's travails and ultimate capture in the Okefenokee Swamp. When the reader considers the intense physical pain that Hiro endures in the swamp, which includes extreme exhaustion and "small shapeless things [that] clung thickly to his calves and thighs" (336), he or she recognizes the pettiness of Ruth's concerns and those of all the writers in residence at Thanatopsis House. In her *New York Times* review of *East Is East*, Gail Godwin describes Boyle's characterization of these writers as follows:

> Ruth's fellow guests at Thanatopsis House include Irving Thalamus, that one-man institution of Jewish-American letters; the haunted, hollow-cheeked Laura Grobian, doyenne of WASP novelists, who sits in a corner with her sherry and a notebook and worries aloud in a voice of "exotic ruination" about the mass suicides at Masada and Jonestown

and Saipan; and the austere, Serious Writer Peter Anserine, who reads European books ("never in translation") at the silent table during meals. . . . Mr. Boyle has fun here, yet the members of his gallery of artists are never just cartoon figures.[10]

The writers in residence at Thanatopsis House are well-rounded characters, and many of them express concern about social issues, but they all appear extremely self-absorbed and distanced from the social problems that affect their own country, including Hiro's travails. Their texts, therefore, are socially disengaged, unlike Boyle's novel *East Is East*, which exposes racial stereotypes and institutionalized racism.

At the end of the novel, Ruth attains the success she so desires. Receiving calls from an agent, Marker McGill, and institutions such as "the *New York Times*, the *San Francisco Chronicle*, the Atlanta, Savannah and Charleston papers, CBS Radio and Mr. Shikuma of the Japan-America Society," Ruth "began to warm to the prospect of a book on Hiro and had even begun to daydream about the amount of the advance and what she would do with it" (353). McGill eventually secures "an offer from a major publisher . . . for a $500,000 advance against a fifteen percent royalty, first serial rights going to one of the leading women's magazines . . . for $75,000, to run in three installments" (356). She has wealth and a publishing contract, and Jane Shine is dead as a result of a freak accident. Her success, however, comes at the price of her final exploitation of Hiro.

At the conclusion of the novel, the dishonored Hiro commits seppuku—ritual samurai suicide—rather than be shipped back to Japan in disgrace. This action is more tragic than heroic. Not only is Hiro led astray by the promise of racial equality in America and betrayed by the one American who befriends him, but he also remains lost in the illusions of the samurai code. He is lost in a sea of texts that include American popular culture, Mishima's *The Way of the Samurai*, and Ruth's upcoming book. With this bleak ending, Boyle does not hold out hope for a means of overcoming racial intolerance and presents the heroism of the samurai as a ridiculous response.

The Road to Wellville (1993)

On his Web site, *TCBoyle.com*, Boyle writes that *The Road to Wellville* was published in 1993 and, until the publication of *The Tortilla Curtain*, was his most widely read book.[11] It is easy to see why Boyle's fifth novel achieved such popularity. *The Road to Wellville* contains a rich cast of satiric characters who participate in one of Boyle's funniest stories. The novel, which Boyle primarily sets in Dr. John Harvey Kellogg's sanitarium (or "the San," as the characters call it) in Battle Creek, Michigan, in 1907 and 1908, vividly captures a period of American history when the country's fascination with health food, exercise, and longevity resembles contemporary America's similar fascination. *The Road to Wellville*, on the surface, returns Boyle to the satiric style of *Water Music* and *Budding Prospects*, the success of which depends upon his virtuosic ability to entertain his readers with a series of outlandishly comic events. But, in actuality *The Road to Wellville* continues Boyle's streak of socially aware fictions by exploring the ways in which authority functions in American society and considering the transformation of progressive idealism into authoritarianism. The founder of biologic living, Dr. John Harvey Kellogg, is the first in a line of Boyle reformers whose idealistic beliefs become the foundation of authoritarian institutions that allow them to determine the lives of other characters who willingly surrender their individuality and become followers.

Because *The Road to Wellville* functions primarily as a satire, it is important to discuss it by analyzing its major characters, who serve as satiric types in the system of the San. These characters include the superintendent of the San, Dr. John Harvey Kellogg; his adopted, estranged, rebellious, poor, and unhealthy son, George; Will and Eleanor Lightbody, an ailing husband and wife from Peterskill, New York, who travel to the San to recover from their disorders; and a potential breakfast-food entrepreneur who also hails from the Peterskill area, Charlie Ossining.

The historical Dr. John Harvey Kellogg was born on 26 February 1852 in Tyrone, New York, and died on 14 December 1943 in Battle Creek, Michigan.[12] A medical doctor, Kellogg took over as superintendent of the Western Health Reform Institute, which had been founded in 1866 on the health principles advocated by the Seventh-day Adventist Church in Battle Creek, Michigan, in 1876 and changed its name to the Battle Creek Sanitarium.[13] At the San, Kellogg practiced holistic medicine, with an emphasis on nutrition, enemas, exercise, and vegetarianism. He was also an inventor, his most popular creations being the cornflake breakfast cereal, peanut butter, and the electric blanket.[14]

In *The Road to Wellville*, Boyle satirizes Kellogg's program of holistic medicine, which he mockingly refers to as "biologic [and/or] physiologic living," and, in so doing, ridicules the dictatorial strategies with which Kellogg wields his authority over the residents of the San. Boyle uses the skeptical Will Lightbody, who is suffering from digestive problems and recovering from alcoholism and opium addiction, as a vehicle for satirizing Kellogg's program, which begins with a diagnosis of "autointoxication" and then proceeds to include such treatments as a vegetarian diet, regularly scheduled enemas (five a day, some with soap and water and others with yogurt!), exercise, sinusoidal baths, vibro-therapy (an exercise in which patients gather to laugh together), abstinence from alcohol and sex, and, occasionally, surgery. When Will meets Kellogg for the first time in the lobby of the San, the doctor "suddenly reached out, took hold of Will Light-body by the lips and forced his fingers into his mouth like a horse trader. 'Yes, yes, say "ah" . . . the coated tongue, I knew it! As severe a case of autointoxication as I've ever scene'" (40) and orders him to be taken to his room in a wheelchair. The speed with which Kellogg diagnoses Will indicates that the diagnosis is more a pronouncement of his power than a thoughtful medical decision. Boyle also compares Kellogg to a horse trader to sug-gest that the diagnosis is a capitalist transaction. By diagnosing Will as an autointoxicant and admitting him to the San, Kellogg stands to make money on his suffering. In the system of the San, Will is no more than an animal, a horse that must respond to its master's bidding. The scene of Will's diagnosis inaugurates a novel-length critique of an authoritarian, dehumanizing, and ultimately economically motivated medical system.

The program of treatment that Will endures in the novel reveals the dehumanizing outcomes of Kellogg's authoritarian regime. Kellogg never indicates the scientific basis for his more radical—and, to contemporary readers, more outrageous—treatments. Will's experience in the sinusoidal baths best demon-strates the dehumanizing and dangerous effects of Kellogg's program. In a sinusoidal bath, patients with nervous disorders relax by placing their feet in buckets of water, which an electric current heats. Will and another patient, Homer Praetz, take their sinusoidal baths at the same time under the guidance of an attendant, Alfred. Will notices that something is wrong: "Comprehension seized him like a pair of hot tongs and he was up and out of the chair in a bound, water sloshing, Alfred dancing, Homer Praetz's eyes like hard-boiled eggs, the shelf rattling, the current sizzling" (217). Will saves Alfred, but Homer dies of electrocution.

Later in the novel, when Will shows his distrust for Kellogg and rebels against his authority by sneaking away from the San and joining Charlie Ossining at a local restaurant, the Red Onion, for whiskey, beer, and hamburgers, Kellogg's reaction suggests the extent to which his treatments allow him to exercise his power over his patients. After Will returns to the San drunk and sick from his binge with Charlie, Kellogg catches him with a bottle of whiskey in his room: "The bottle of Old Overholt stood there on the night table, incontrovertible, the half-filled glass behind it. . . . and in the next moment the Doctor was in action, catlike in his quickness, springing across the room to seize the glass and bottle and smash them over the edge of the table so that the floor exploded with jewels of glass and the jagged neck of the bottle, gripped tight, blossomed in the bulb of his fist" (252). Kellogg's violent reaction to the way in which Will corrupts the purity of the San by bringing a bottle of whiskey onto its premises illustrates the irrationality that lies below the surface of his scientific opposition to alcohol. In addition, when Kellogg schedules Will for "'Lane's Kink surgery' . . . to remove a portion of the lower intestine where stasis routinely occurs" right after this rebellion against his authority (253), he is using his authority to concoct a painful way to punish his patient for his misdeeds and keep him subservient, thereby demonstrating the connection between his treatments and power. Will endures many such treatments/punishments in the novel, including painful yogurt enemas.

As David Lipsky has pointed out in his review of *The Road to Wellville*, Kellogg "has fixated on the clenched bowel as the source of ill health,"[15] and most of Kellogg's treatments and policies focus on cleanliness and purity. This emphasis on cleanliness and purity extends to his proclamation of the irreducible connection between sexual abstinence and biologic living, demonstrating itself most prominently in the ways in which he polices the sex lives of his patients. He separates Will and Eleanor when they arrive at the San, criticizing the former when he finds out that he tried to visit his wife in her room: "I happen to know for a fact that on the night of November sixteen, overcome with your sick lusts, you inflicted yourself on your invalid wife, thereby risking her life—her *life*, I say—just as surely as if you'd held a knife to her throat. And you. Look at you. Your vital fluids depleted, your digestion ruined, the rotten scrawl of death written all over you" (194). Upholding the myths that health is related to the retention of seminal and vaginal fluids and that sex is dirty, Kellogg makes Will feel guilty in the early parts of the novel for his attraction both to his wife and to his primary caretaker, Nurse Graves. Craig Seligman, in his review of the novel in the *New Republic*, notes that, as a satirist, Boyle "doesn't show much interest in the psychology of [sexual] repression. He just wants to demonstrate that it's a lousy idea."[16] While Boyle's characterization of the anal retentive Kellogg seems ripe for Freudian analysis, his primary aim is to suggest the extent to which the doctor's authoritarian interventions into the lives of his patients determine their inner lives and external actions.

In addition to satirizing Kellogg for his interest in controlling his patients' bowels, sex lives, and diet, Boyle also reveals how his medical ideals owe more to the performing arts and sales-manship than to hard science. Throughout the novel Kellogg gives a series of lectures at the San that, on the surface, educate his patients about biologic living but, in reality, use theatrics to indoctrinate them into his beliefs and make them subservient to his rule. Boyle begins the novel with one of Kellogg's perfor-mances, in which Kellogg asks one of the patients in attendance, Ida Muntz, to compare "a bit of . . . horse excretus" to "a good sixteen-ounce steak" by analyzing them under a microscope (6). Kellogg argues that the piece of horse excrement and the steak contain the same "unfriendly bacteria, the *B. welchii*, *B. coli* and *Proteus vulgaris* we so often see in the stool of our incoming patients here at the Sanitarium" (11). After Ida verifies that the two samples appear the same under the microscope, Kellogg encourages "an ancient, foul-smelling and fouler-tempered chim-panzee by the name of Lillian" to eat the steak, and her refusal to do so functions as his proof that the consumption of meat "pollut[es] the temple of the human body" (10). Lillian chooses to eat a banana instead of the steak. What Kellogg does not tell his audience is that as a chimpanzee, Lillian naturally prefers bananas to steaks. This scene suggests Kellogg's willingness to forgo the rigors of science and employ deceptive theatrics to advance his power. Like Boyle himself, Kellogg is a master show-man, but Kellogg's theater is dangerous because it deceives peo-ple into surrendering their freedom and creates a mindless legion of followers, whereas Boyle's theater encourages people to ques-tion authority.

Kellogg's fanatical emphasis on sexual abstinence means that he and his wife do not have any biological children of their own. Instead they adopt more than forty children, among whom George is the most important in the novel. The reader meets George in the appropriately titled "Father to All, Father to

None" chapter, when he arrives at the San wanting money on the night of Kellogg's lecture on bacteria in horse excrement and steak. George's appearance—unhealthy, poor, and rebellious—calls into question the principles of biologic living: "George said nothing. He merely slouched there, ragged and twisted, ugly as a turnip, and grinned to show off his yellowed teeth and rotten gums" (36). The Kelloggs adopt George after finding him in Chicago in conditions of squalor: "They found George—he was known only as 'Hildah's boy' then, with neither Christian nor family name attached to him—sitting beside the corpse of his mother in an unheated shack out back of a South Side slum" (42–43). George, however, rejects Kellogg's dictates and the policies of his house, "or the Residence, as it was called" (43), which is structured according to the same orderly and authoritarian principles as the San. "The children," for example, "slept in dormitories according to their ages and sexes, they were attended to and educated by San nurses and staffers, and they were provided with all the plain unvarnished accoutrements of La Vie Simple, from calisthenics in the morning to beet soufflé, okra soup and three-ounce portions of baked Cornlet in the evening" (43). Throughout his life George consistently rebels against the authority of his adoptive parents, loudly passing gas during a Christmas recital, demanding meat and potatoes during a meal, becoming a partner in the Per-Fo breakfast cereal company with Charlie Ossining and Goodloe Bender, and eventually attempting to burn down the San itself. But the best example of his rebellious nature occurs when he, as a small boy, refuses to hang up his jacket in the manner that Kellogg desires. Kellogg punishes George by forcing him to hang up his jacket in the desired manner repeatedly for a long period of time. After this period of time elapses and Kellogg tells him that the punishment is sufficient,

George ignores him and continues to perform the procedure, exasperating his father and provoking a violent reaction: "Grunting with the effort, he tore the jacket from the boy's shoulders, tore it to pieces, and then, in the pale light of the moon in the still and shadowy hall, he slapped that unyielding little wedge of a face till his hand was raw" (49). This scene not only reveals the ineffectual impact of biologic living on George but also the irrational and hypocritical violence that resides just beneath the surface of Kellogg's rational and scientific exterior.

Unlike George and unlike her husband, Will, Eleanor Lightbody begins the novel as a true believer in Kellogg's ideals. Pained by the death of her newborn daughter and by Will's recent bouts with alcoholism and opium addiction, Eleanor arrives at the San willing to participate in Kellogg's treatment program and to surrender her freedom to him. But like her husband, she eventually decides to rebel against his tenets. Eleanor rebels when she falls under the influence of a fellow patient named Lionel Badger, who tells her and other patients, including a shocked Will and Charlie's aunt Mrs. Hookstratten, about a controversial New Jersey commune, Helicon Home: "*I* was there at Helicon Home, and I can assure you, madame, that the experiment in communal living was a noble and progressive one" (354). When Mrs. Hookstratten responds to Badger's claim by arguing that "there were accusations of all sorts of improper goings-on there . . . of sun worship, and nudity, free love" (354), she could be reiterating Kellogg's own notions of sexual morality. But Badger counters by linking the practices of Helicon Home to women's rights: "The man is free to indulge his whims, but if a woman should presume to take a lover, why, the president wouldn't be able to sleep at night" (355). This argument immediately appeals to Eleanor, who has already taken Badger's

advice and secretly visited the mysterious Dr. Spitzvogel, a graduate of "the Universität of Schleswig-Holstein" and, as he tells
Eleanor during their first meeting, practitioner of "the Philosophy of Physiological Systems, and, of course, Therapeutic
Massage—*Die Handhabung Therapeutik*, in particular" (346).
In Boyle's comic description, Spitzvogel manipulates Eleanor's
womb during the massage—that is, brings her to orgasm for the
first time in her life: "So delicate, so painstaking, so exquisite in
its patience and deep probing wisdom, this was a touch she
could never have conjured or imagined" (348). When Kellogg
finds out about Eleanor's sessions with Spitzvogel, he gets angry
with her for visiting another doctor. Eleanor questions Kellogg's
authority by visiting Spitzvogel and continues to do so by
defending womb manipulation when the superintendent of the
San confronts her about it, announcing that she "never felt better in [her] life" (392).

Just because Eleanor rebels against Kellogg's authority in her
association with Badger and Spitzvogel does not mean that Boyle
endorses their beliefs. As usual, in the novel Boyle uses Will to
provide a skeptical perspective on free love and womb manipulation. In the scene in which Badger defends Helicon Home, Will
remembers that the commune's success depended upon the way
in which it was promoted in the newspapers: "The press made a
big to-do over the issue of free love . . . and titillated readers
throughout the Hudson Valley and beyond with visions of midnight rendezvous and wives available for the asking" (354). In a
striking reminder of Kellogg's theatrical approach to science,
Will realizes that the central tenets of Helicon Home achieve
notoriety not because of their scientific truth, but because of the
way in which the press glorifies them. Similarly skeptical about
Spitzvogel, Will late in the novel discovers the doctor, Badger,

Eleanor, and Virginia Cranehill (another San patient), as they engage in a womb manipulation session in the woods near the San: "[Spitzvogel's] arms were extended on each side of him, his hands working between the women's legs. The other man— it was Badger—stood just behind them, masturbating himself" (432). As Will attacks Badger with a stick that he wields as a "baseball bat," the reader realizes that Badger and perhaps even Spitzvogel himself use their so-called scientific theories to advance their own interests and gain sexual gratification. This realization allows the reader to connect Badger and Spitzvogel to Kellogg as authoritarian quacks who selfishly accumulate power over other people.

As he does with Felix and Petra in *Budding Prospects* and Tom and Jessica in *World's End*, Boyle in *The Road to Wellville* posits heterosexual monogamy as the true means of rejecting authoritarians such as Kellogg. Kellogg opposes sex, even between married heterosexual couples. It is no wonder, then, that both Eleanor and Will rebel against Kellogg's authority in their sex lives. Eleanor rebels by exploring the sexual pseudo-philosophies of Badger and Spitzvogel. The "increasingly randy" Will, in turn, rebels by donning an electric "Heidelberg Belt," which he wears on his penis to improve his sexual potency and relieve nervous tension, and by attempting to seduce Nurse Graves (352). But when Will arrives to save Eleanor from Badger and Spitzvogel in a parody of heroic climactic scenes in Victorian novels, the Lightbodys deny their experiments with quack treatments and sexual infidelity. After Will trounces his enemies, he looks at the naked Eleanor and finds "himself growing hard as he watched her, harder than any mail-order belt or buxom nurse could ever make him" (434). Just as Will's sexual potency is restored, Eleanor, the reader discovers in the coda to the novel, gives birth to three daughters and becomes "president of the Peterskill chapter of the National American Woman Suffrage Association and in 1919 travel[s] throughout the country lobbying for passage of the Nineteenth Amendment" (472–73). Restored to her marriage with Will, Eleanor no longer holds that Kellogg's program for biologic living can save the world and now believes that salvation came through "basic human rights, it was education, it was a giving and a selfless devotion to the cause" (472). Eleanor's decision to uphold a more moderate approach to biologic living and dedicate herself to issues of social justice reflects Boyle's judgment that Kellogg's methods are ultimately selfish.

Boyle uses the character of Charlie Ossining to offer a second means of surviving an America dominated by quackery and authoritarianism. When Charlie arrives in Battle Creek at the beginning of the novel, he models himself on C. W. Post, the breakfast-food magnate who "made his first million by 1901" (75), and desires to start producing his own cereal, Per-Fo, which his business card describes as *The 'Perfect Food,' Predigested, Peptonized and Celery Impregnated. Perks Up Tired Blood and Exonerates the Bowels*" (23). Charlie already has $3,849.55 of Mrs. Hookstratten's money invested in his disgusting, celery-based product, and he eventually augments this sum with a $1,000 investment courtesy of Will Lightbody and yet another investment by Mrs. Hookstratten. Recalling Ned Rise from *Water Music*, Charlie is essentially a con man who is primarily concerned with his own survival and is willing to cheat and lie in order to become rich. He struggles throughout the novel to start producing Per-Fo cereal, partnering with George Kellogg so that he can use the Kellogg name to sell his product, filling cereal boxes bearing the Per-Fo label with cereal made by a rival company, getting Will Lightbody and Mrs. Hookstratten to invest in a nonexistent product, and avoiding detection by the police when his other business partner, Goodloe Bender, skips town with their investments and without having paid his expensive hotel bills. Near the conclusion of the novel, Kellogg, in his typically theatrical manner, denounces Charlie, Charlie's endeavor to use the Kellogg name to sell Per-Fo, and the worldview he represents before a crowd of San patients (423). Aware of Kellogg's hypocritical reference to his son George and his inability to recognize the ways in which he himself deceives his patients, the reader sides with Charlie in this moment and is satisfied when he escapes the police in a freak carriage accident, changes his name to "Charles Peter McGahee" (468), and becomes rich making "Per-To," "a specific for pleurisy, heart ailments, diphtheria, the flu, general weakness, men's troubles, women's troubles and rectal itch" that contains "a forty-percent-alcohol solution ('Added Solely as a Solvent and Preservative')" (469–70). Like Ned Rise in *Water Music*, Charlie experiences a lucky break that allows him to achieve his dream, with Boyle suggesting that being true to oneself is one of the novel's central moral arguments.

The death of George Kellogg at the novel's conclusion emphasizes this moral argument. An unrepentant rebel, George sets fire to the San in an ultimate defiance of his father's authority but falls into a giant vat of macadamia-nut butter in the San's experimental kitchens when his father savagely beats him. The butter, which is "smooth and nutritious and replete enough to restore three-quarters of the stomachs in Battle Creek" (461–62), does not restore George to health; rather, Kellogg uses it to drown his son: "he held the boy's face there and fought it down with every ounce of outraged physiologic strength he could summon even as it lashed to the surface shrieking for air and fell back again into the oleaginous grip of the stuff" (462). With Kellogg's prized health food serving as the weapon in the murder of his son, Boyle reveals the reality of the irrational hate that overcomes Kellogg's scientific dedication to the prolongation of life. Like many Boyle characters, Kellogg descends to a state of animality and asserts his physical prowess: "He was John Harvey Kellogg, and he would live forever" (463). Death, however, has the final word, and Boyle concludes the novel by writing, "On December 14, 1943, like his nemesis C. W. Post before him, John Harvey Kellogg passed on into eternity. He did die, yes. But could anyone ask for more?" (476). Despite all his attempts to thwart death through science and biologic living, Kellogg dies, and nature provides him with the ultimate punishment for his hypocrisies and authoritarianism.

Mark Schechner, in his review in the *Buffalo News*, considers the ways in which *The Road to Wellville* comments not only on the America of 1907 and 1908 but on contemporary America as well: "the sinusoidal bath . . . has had a recent revival among sports therapists; vegetarianism has never been more in vogue, and sexual abstinence is making a comeback."[17] *The Road to Wellville*, by extension, can be read as a critique of both the historical and contemporary willingness of Americans to surrender their freedom to hypocritical leaders who state their intentions to work for the people's needs but may in reality be more interested in increasing their own personal power. Boyle employs his satire to encourage Americans to think critically about their leaders and social systems—to be always on the lookout for the authoritarian hypocrites in their midst.

The Tortilla Curtain (1995)

Boyle published his sixth and most controversial novel, *The Tortilla Curtain*, in 1995, and he introduces it on his Web site as follows:

> Because it dealt with a hot-button socio-political issue—
> illegal immigration in Southern California—many of the
> reviewers came into the book with strong prejudices. I took
> a good deal of abuse, including (my favorite instance) being
> called "human garbage" on a call-in radio show in San
> Francisco. As people have had a chance to think more
> deeply over the course of the past few years, the furor has
> died down and *The Tortilla Curtain* has become a modern
> classic, by far my most popular title, widely read in high
> schools and universities around the country.[18]

The Tortilla Curtain is Boyle's most controversial novel for three reasons. First, in writing about a "hot-button socio-political issue" about which many people have strong opinions, Boyle chooses a subject matter that risks alienating some readers. Second, Boyle's serious approach to illegal immigration makes *The Tortilla Curtain* his least comic work to date. His first novel on illegal immigration, *East Is East*, is in his more familiar dark comic style, making it more accessible to readers already familiar with his work. Third, Boyle writes *The Tortilla Curtain* from the perspectives of four characters living in the Topanga Canyon area on the outskirts of Los Angeles, California, two of whom, Delaney and Kyra Mossbacher, are wealthy, affluent, and white American citizens, and two of whom, Cándido and América Rincón, are poor Mexican migrant workers. Some critics and readers have taken issue with what they perceive to be Boyle's audacious and politically irresponsible decision to write from the perspective of members of a minority culture.

Boyle crafts a profoundly unsettling novel, one that causes his readers to examine and evaluate their own opinions on race and illegal immigration. Perhaps the most unsettling aspect of *The Tortilla Curtain* to many of Boyle's American readers is the way in which it presents Delaney Mossbacher's descent into racism. Delaney, at the beginning of the novel, is a forty-something "liberal humanist with an unblemished driving record and a freshly waxed Japanese car with personalized plates" (3). Boyle contrasts Delaney's materialism to his progressive political beliefs, which resemble those of Tom and Jessica in *World's End*. Delaney is a former participant in antinuclear demonstrations, who earns his living by writing a column, "Pilgrim at Topanga Creek," for the environmentalist magazine *Wide Open Spaces* and who works as a homemaker for his wife, Kyra, and six-year-old stepson, Jordan, while Kyra pursues her career as a successful real-estate agent. Despite these progressive beliefs and actions, Delaney lives in an affluent and exclusive community in Topanga Canyon, Arroyo Blanco Estates, and as Heather J. Hicks has argued, his material possessions define him as an individual and, more important for a novel on race relations and illegal immigration, as a member of the white race.[19] As the novel progresses, the reader realizes that regardless of his professed progressive values, Delaney is blind to his privileged social status as a white American. The novel presents Delaney with many opportunities to act on his progressive values and to answer a question that Boyle himself posed in an interview with David Appell: "[Delaney's] a liberal, sure, but is he willing to act on it when the time comes?"[20]

Delaney's first opportunity to act on his progressive values occurs when he hits Cándido with his brand new Acura. After the accident, in a scene reminiscent of Saxby and Ruth's first encounter with Hiro in *East Is East*, Delaney and Cándido cannot communicate effectively because of the language barrier—the former speaks only English and the latter speaks only Spanish. Delaney eventually gives Cándido twenty dollars in cash, and after he thinks about the incident later in the chapter, "his guilt turn[s] to anger, to outrage" (11). Delaney is upset, not because he feels remorse for hitting Cándido with his car, but because he assumes (correctly) that Cándido lives in the Topanga Canyon State Park: "Making the trees and bushes and the natural habitat of Topanga State Park into his own private domicile, crapping in the chaparral, dumping his trash behind rocks, polluting the stream and ruining it for everyone else. That was state property down there, rescued from the developers and their bulldozers and set aside for the use of the public, for nature, not for some outdoor ghetto" (11). In his study of the influence of Mike Davis's book *The Ecology of Fear: Los Angeles and the Imagination of Disaster* on *The Tortilla Curtain*, Gregory Meyerson notes, "The liberal motif of preserving public space from the developers, a real concern in L.A. as Davis shows, is here trumped by a virulent racism (of which Delaney is largely unaware) that blames poor people for pollution."[21] Delaney is unaware that his environmentalism contributes to his underlying racist attitudes toward poor Mexican migrant workers. Even though Delaney does not connect his environmentalism to his racist attitudes in this early scene, he at least recognizes the contradiction between giving Cándido the twenty dollars and his progressive beliefs: "he'd just left the poor son of a bitch there alongside the road, abandoned him, and because he'd been glad of it, relieved to buy him off with his twenty dollars' blood money. And how did that square with his liberal-humanist ideals?" (13).

Early in the novel, Delaney is able to pose the tough question that Boyle himself asks in his interview with David Appell. But as the novel continues, Delaney loses this ability, his attitudes becoming progressively more racist and intolerant. Boyle traces Delaney's descent into racism by contrasting the Mossbachers' experiences to the Rincóns' experiences. He employs this method to reveal the superficiality of the affluent and wealthy Mossbachers' lives in relation to the extreme poverty, physical pain, and existential uncertainty that characterize the Rincóns' lives.

The best way to understand Boyle's narrative structure in *The Tortilla Curtain* is to compare the Delaney narrative to the Cándido narrative. The first point of comparison is the names "Delaney Mossbacher" and "Cándido Rincón." Geraldine Stoneham notes that "Delaney Mossbacher" is a hybrid name, one that is of both Irish and German ancestry.[22] Delaney's name immediately suggests the extent to which the white citizens of the United States come from mixed immigrant ancestries. In addition the name "Mossbacher," according to Peter Freese, resembles the word "mossback," which signifies an entrenched conservative who does not think for himself.[23] Delaney professes progressive attitudes and, by all appearances, lives a progressive lifestyle. As the novel progresses, however, Delaney begins to reflect the conservative philosophies of his neighbor Jack Jardine. When Delaney argues to Jack that "immigrants are the lifeblood of this country—we're a nation of immigrants—and neither of us would be standing here today if it wasn't" (101),

Jack responds by making an economic argument: "The illegals in San Diego County contributed seventy million in tax revenues and at the same time they used up two hundred and forty million in services—welfare, emergency care, schooling and the like. You want to pay for that? And for the crime that comes with it?" (102). Later in the novel, Delaney, who originally opposes Jack's proposal to construct a wall around Arroyo Blanco Estates to deter crime and keep out illegal immigrants, does not intervene when he witnesses Cándido being assaulted by a truck driver and wrongly accuses another Mexican migrant worker of trespassing in his neighborhood. These actions reveal Delaney's hypocrisy in his profession of progressive values, a hypocrisy heightened by his name, which alludes to the immigrant experience that makes possible his privileged existence in America.

In Spanish, Cándido Rincón's first name means "naive," and his last name connotes "corner or nook." In addition, as Elisabeth Schäfer-Wünsche has posited, Boyle gives his chief Mexican migrant worker the first name "Cándido" to refer to the eponymous hero of Voltaire's novel *Candide*, who haplessly travels in search of the best of all possible worlds.[24] Boyle constructs Cándido as a naive traveler who eventually finds that, despite what he has heard about the mythic "wide open spaces" of America, his race traps him in many corners when he tries to make his living in the Topanga Canyon area, most prominently on the canyon floor where he and América make their home. Unlike Delaney, whose race ensures that he can pursue and benefit from the American dream regardless of his immigrant ancestry, Cándido's race makes it difficult for him to find a similar success and sense of belonging.

Roland Walter's argument that *The Tortilla Curtain* renders "an up-to-date version of the American Dream as a living myth distorted by a self-serving dynamic . . . that affirms Anglo-American identity" illuminates Boyle's reason for writing the novel from the perspectives of the two couples.[25] The common experiences of the Mossbachers and Rincóns demonstrate their common humanity. Not only does Delaney hit Cándido with his Acura at the beginning of the novel, but both also shop at the same grocery store, are married to independent and strong women, enjoy drinking beer, cook a turkey on Thanksgiving, and live in the same section of Los Angeles. But despite these commonalities, Delaney and Cándido are separated by poverty and race. Delaney and Cándido do shop at the same grocery store, but the former purchases ingredients for the pricey meals that he prepares for Kyra and Jordan, whereas the latter is lucky if he has enough money to afford basic staples such as beans and tortillas and is occasionally forced to eat garbage. Whereas Delaney decides to live in an expensive home in an exclusive community in the unspoiled nature of Topanga Canyon, Cándido is forced to live in a temporary camp on the floor of the canyon. Whereas Delaney perceives nature as a benign but theoretically dangerous inspiration for his magazine column and a place for him to hike at his convenience, Cándido's poverty compels him to live in nature and to know the reality of searching for water and food in the unforgiving weather of a Southern California summer. Whereas Delaney's race allows him to walk freely the streets of his community, Cándido's race obliges him to look out constantly for the INS agents who threaten to arrest him as an illegal immigrant. Whereas Delaney, as the recipient of a considerable inheritance from his parents, only works because he wants to, Cándido must work to survive. And whereas Delaney routinely retreats to his study for a few hours a day to write his column, Cándido seeks work everyday as a menial laborer just so that he can have enough money to feed América and himself and possibly save for an apartment.

Delaney, Jack, and other white characters in the novel use race as a signifier of social acceptance and material wealth. When Delaney sees a Mexican in his neighborhood, he immediately feels aggravated and threatened: "[the man] was crossing the Cherrystones' lawn with the lingering insouciant stride of the trespasser. . . . And then Delaney came closer still, and noticed something else, something that struck him with the force of a blow: the man was Mexican" (228). Delaney uses the Mexican's skin color to identify him as the character the reader knows as Jose Navidad, "the hiker, the illegal camper" who bothered him on one of his hiking trips and who "threatened [Kyra] at the Da Ros place" (228). Delaney accuses the Mexican of trespassing, only to learn that he has been hired to deliver fliers. Delaney's accusation is particularly unsettling because he makes it right after he indicates his opposition to the construction of the wall to Todd Sweet, another opponent of the wall, who, like the Mexican deliverer of fliers, is visiting the houses in the neighborhood. Delaney, of course, is not similarly afraid when he sees Todd because Todd is white. He tells Todd, "The idea of a wall is completely and utterly offensive" (226), but he still uses skin color as the impetus for his desire to exclude the Mexican worker from the neighborhood in which he owns property.

The wall functions as a controversial social issue that provokes strong reactions in the white community. Boyle uses Delaney's changing reactions to the wall—first he opposes the wall, and then he favors it because it "would . . . keep burglars, rapists, graffiti artists and coyotes out of the development" and make the environment of Topanga Canyon "his own private nature preserve" (245–46)—to trace the process by which the reality of his racism overcomes his progressive statements on immigration. In his interview with David Appell, Boyle stated that Delaney's actions are "an anatomy of what racism and scapegoating are."[26] When Delaney purchases a new Acura at the beginning of the novel, Boyle writes, "That was the American way. Buy something. Feel good. But [Delaney] didn't feel good, not at all. He felt like a victim" (149). As the novel progresses, Kyra tells Delaney about Jose Navidad's harassment of her, and Jose Navidad harasses Delaney himself on one of his hiking trips. These events, coupled with the way in which Delaney blames the Mexicans for the pollution of the Topanga Canyon State Park, heighten his feeling of victimization. Boyle suggests that Delaney's feeling of victimization is an irrational response to the actions of individual men such as Jose Navidad. From his irrational feeling of victimization, Delaney proceeds to an equally irrational anger against all Mexicans, which his behavior in the closing sections of the novel best exemplifies. Delaney stakes out a section of the newly constructed wall in the hopes of taking pictures of vandals who have spray painted racial slurs against white people on the wall and set the fire that engulfs Topanga Canyon. He expects his picture to prove that Jose Navidad is the perpetrator, but the picture instead shows the "silver-flecked moustache, the crushed cheekbone" of Cándido (320). Even though the picture does not reveal Cándido in the act of spray painting the slurs and the reader knows that he is innocent, Delaney takes a gun and races out to catch him, illustrating the extent to which his racism causes him to become irrationally violent and, in a reiteration of a theme that occupies Boyle starting with the *Descent of Man* collection and links many of his works, to descend to a state of animality.

Delaney's action in this scene appears even more violent and irrational because of Boyle's use of multiple narrative perspectives and styles. Heike Paul notes that Boyle renders the Mossbacher narrative in his more familiar, satiric style, whereas he presents the Rincón narrative in a more dramatic and even tragic tone.[27] Boyle's narrative decision gives the Rincóns more depth as characters than the Mossbachers. Both Cándido and América remember dehumanizing events from their lives, including Cándido's first trips to work in America, his betrayal by his first wife, Resurrección, his experiences avoiding the INS, and the attempted rape of América at the border. Boyle does not grant the Mossbachers—or any of the white characters in the novel, for that matter—similar memories; he, instead, provides brief glimpses into their past, such as Kyra's first marriage and Delaney's social activism. Because they do not have painful experiences similar to the Rincóns', the Mossbachers appear extremely superficial and less authentic. Boyle points out this superficiality when he introduces the Mossbachers by depicting a typical morning in their lives in the third chapter of the novel: "Kyra insisted on the full nutritional slate for her son every morning—fresh fruit, granola with skim milk and brewer's yeast, hi-fiber bar. The child needed roughage. Vitamins. Whole grains. And breakfast, for a growing child at least, was the most important meal of the day, the foundation of all that was to come" (34). Kyra's thoughts on the importance of breakfast and the way in which she spoils her son provide a sharp contrast to the poor Rincóns, who are lucky to make enough money doing menial labor just to survive. América thinks, "The beans were gone, the *tortillas*, the lard, the last few grains of rice. And what were they going to eat—grass? Like the cows?" (80). Despite their membership in such progressive organizations as "the Sierra Club, Save the Children, the National Wildlife Foundation and the Democratic Party" (34), the Mossbachers are completely removed from the reality of the Rincóns' suffering. Delaney and Kyra *do* suffer in the novel, the former when he hits Cándido with his Acura and his replacement car is stolen and the latter when coyotes steal her dogs and she experiences difficulty selling the Da Ros home, but this suffering seems petty when compared to that of the Rincóns. Boyle complicates the Mossbachers' suffering by bringing them into contact with Jose Navidad, who harasses both Delaney, when he is on one of his hiking trips, and Kyra, when she locks up the Da Ros property one night. But the overwhelming sense is that the Mossbachers, despite their membership in progressive organizations, live petty insular lives that desensitize them to the suffering that goes on all around them. This lack of sensitivity results in Kyra's opposition to the Labor Exchange and both Mossbachers' support of the wall in Arroyo Blanco Estates.

Two other prominent twentieth-century American novels of political engagement, John Steinbeck's *The Grapes of Wrath* (1939) and William Faulkner's *Light in August* (1932), influenced Boyle in *The Tortilla Curtain*. Boyle specifically refers to another Steinbeck novel, *Tortilla Flat* (1935), in the title of his novel and uses an excerpt from *The Grapes of Wrath*—"They ain't human. A human being wouldn't live like they do. A human being couldn't stand it to be so dirty and miserable"—as an epigraph. These references ask readers to keep in mind Steinbeck's novels and left-wing politics as they read *The Tortilla Curtain*, prompting them to equate the suffering of the Joad family in *The Grapes of Wrath* to that of Cándido and América. When seen in the context of *The Grapes of Wrath* and other leftist

Steinbeck novels, *The Tortilla Curtain* becomes a text that supports the rights of Mexican immigrants and criticizes so-called liberal American citizens who favor the accumulation of material possessions at the expense of political engagement.

In addition to Steinbeck's novels, in *The Tortilla Curtain* Boyle also refers to *Light in August*, most prominently in the character of Jose Navidad, whose name is a Spanish translation of the name of Faulkner's character, Joe Christmas. Both Gregory Meyerson and Heather J. Hicks note Boyle's reference to Joe Christmas,[28] whose mysterious racial identity is white and black, perhaps even Mexican. Because of this mixed racial identity, Christmas feels impure, punished by God, and alienated from society, and his violent nature derives partially from the anger that results from his racial difference. Hicks writes,

> Boyle's choice to borrow Christmas is compelling because it signals a number of major historical shifts and continuations within the story of twentieth-century racial thinking. Indeed, tracing the debate within the course of Faulkner's novel as to whether Christmas's father was Mexican rather than black suggests that, should Christmas have been determined to have been of Mexican descent, he would have been spared much of both the self-directed and the external animosity that he suffers in his life. In reconceiving Joe Christmas as part Mexican in a new time and region of the United States, Boyle reminds the reader of the contingency of racial status. The novel suggests that as a consequence of shifting social dynamics, Mexicans in late-twentieth-century Southern California are now assigned a racial designation once reserved for blacks, and Navidad is hated accordingly.[29]

Hicks's analysis highlights that race in *The Tortilla Curtain* is a social construction and suggests that white Southern Californians treat Mexicans with the same ire that white Americans reserved for African Americans in Faulkner's era. Jose Navidad, like Joe Christmas, is not innocent of reprehensible actions, his most heinous crime being his rape of América. But, as Hicks argues, "Navidad's transgressions and the responses they inspire suggest that the lifeblood, as it were, of contemporary whiteness is not blood at all, but material property. If control is the metaphysical condition of whiteness, material property is its physical expression."[30] By committing such "transgressive" actions as entering the property of the Da Ros home and camping in Delaney's private nature preserve of Topanga Canyon, Jose Navidad threatens the material property of white people that is the primary component in the construction of whiteness. Boyle's inclusion in *The Tortilla Curtain* of Jose Navidad, a character who specifically refers to Faulkner's depiction of racism and racial construction in *Light in August*, indicates his presentation of race as a social construct that some white Americans use to consolidate their power over other races.

Read in the context of Boyle's critique of white America's social construction of race, the ending of *The Tortilla Curtain* is very appropriate to his overriding political message. By the end of the novel, Cándido is Delaney's scapegoat for many offenses, including the spray-painted racial slurs on the Arroyo Blanco Estates wall, the pollution in the Topanga Canyon State Park, and the Topanga Canyon fire, which Cándido starts when he attempts to roast a frozen turkey on Thanksgiving Day. Gregory Meyerson reports that the fire, which resembles the historical Old Topanga Fire of November 1993, is "a natural part of the chaparral ecology and it would have happened at this time of year with or without the turkey since the Santa Anas are strongest during the fall, especially between Labor Day and Thanksgiving."[31] As a nature writer, Delaney is aware of the region's ecology, but his irrational racial hatred causes him to accuse Cándido of starting the fire anyway and to pursue him with a gun. When Delaney locates his prey, a mudslide occurs that threatens to destroy everything in its path. Despite the fact that his baby girl dies in the mudslide, Cándido, in a melodramatic ending reminiscent of Victorian novels, saves Delaney from drowning: "But when he saw the white face surge up out of the black swirl of the current and the white hand grasping at the tiles, he reached down and took hold of it" (355). In this closing sentence, Cándido saves his enemy and demonstrates the common humanity that transcends race and class. Despite all Cándido's suffering as a poor Mexican migrant worker and all his understandable reasons for hating his chief tormentor, he overcomes his anger and loves his enemy.

Riven Rock (1998)

Boyle sets *Riven Rock*, his seventh novel, in the same time period as *The Road to Wellville*.[32] Taking place mainly between 1908 and 1928, *Riven Rock* covers much of the same thematic territory as the earlier novel, including most prominently the treatment and dehumanization of the ill. *Riven Rock*, however, differs from its predecessor by focusing on mental illness, a condition that it examines through the lens of a historical couple: Stanley and Katherine McCormick. The wealthy son of Cyrus McCormick, the inventor of the mechanical reaper and founder of the International Harvester Company, Stanley begins behaving oddly shortly after his marriage to Katherine in 1904 and is eventually confined to his family's estate at Riven Rock (which is located close to Boyle's home in Santa Barbara) as a paranoid schizophrenic, sexual maniac, and violent misogynist. Stanley's wife, Katherine, who is today remembered as one of the first female graduates of the Massachusetts Institute of Technology, a leader in the National American Woman Suffrage Association that worked to secure voting rights for women, and an important early proponent of diaphragms and the birth control pill, remains loyal to him throughout his period of institutionalization, which lasts from shortly after their marriage until his death in 1947. In a 1998 interview with Laura Reynolds Adler, Boyle noted that telling the story of the McCormicks' marriage "was a way to talk about the division of the sexes in America, particularly from the turn of the century on, when the women's movement was starting to evolve. It was a way to talk about fidelity in a relationship, to talk about sex in a relationship, to talk about marriage."[33] Boyle elaborates on his intentions in rendering the McCormicks' marriage in his Web site's introduction to *Riven Rock*: "This is a love story, grand, depressing, and, I hope, ultimately touching."[34]

The structure of *Riven Rock* is instrumental to its discussion of women's rights, its critique of the treatment of the mentally ill, and its love story. The three main sections of the novel—"Dr. Hamilton's Time," "Dr. Brush's Time," and "Dr. Kempf's Time"—correspond to the time periods during which Stanley's three main psychiatrists care for him. These psychiatrists have different approaches to Stanley's treatment, but they all agree that because of his violent urges and uncontrollable sexual desires, he needs to be isolated—as the title of the novel's prologue, "World without Women," indicates—under the care of an exclusively male staff. With his interest in trying to discover the origin of Stanley's illness and his research into human sexual behavior in the behavior of primates (a zoo of which he keeps at Riven Rock for his research purposes), Dr. Hamilton represents the behavioral approach. Eddie O'Kane, one of Stanley's nurses and a typical Boyle worldly-wise con man who recalls Ned Rise from *Water Music* and Charlie Ossining from *The Road to Wellville*, skeptically assesses Hamilton's research as he attempts to locate a missing Stanley: "O'Kane had observed enough of the doctor's experiments by now to form an opinion, and his opinion was that they were bunk. Aside from running the monkeys through the big wooden box with the gates in it, all Hamilton and his seedy-looking assistants seemed to do was make the monkeys fuck one another—or anything else that came to hand" (154). Eddie eventually finds Stanley in a grove of trees: "These were no monkeys, but apes, the rutilant naked one, white as any ghost, and the shaggy hunkering split-faced one, and their hands moving each at the place where the other's legs intersected, two hands flashing in that obscene light until O'Kane, who now truly had seen everything, flicked it off" (155). Hamilton's treatment does not improve Stanley's condition, which manifests itself in an inability to control sexual urges; rather, it exasperates it, remaking it as scientific evidence for Stanley's animality and, by extension, for the animality of all humans. Boyle indicates the dehumanizing way in which the medical establishment transforms patients from people into, as Eddie puts it, "grist for [the] theoretical mill" of scientific discourse and power (154).

Both Dr. Brush and Dr. Kempf are equally ineffective in treating Stanley. Like Hamilton, they keep their patient confined at Riven Rock, but their therapeutic approach differs from their predecessor's. Brush and Kempf are Freudian believers in the "talking cure," and their psychoanalytic theories influence their treatment of Stanley and reflect a transformation in the treatment of the mentally ill that occurred in America after Freud's theories became popular. Brush begins a typical session with Stanley by asking him, "How are you this fine morning?" and telling him that he is "the lucky one to have such fine weather here all the year round" (235–36). When Stanley replies that he feels "no luckier than a dog" (236), Brush wants to find out why Stanley chooses the word "dog" to describe his feelings. In this scene and the rest of the scenes in which Stanley undergoes treatment by Brush or Kempf, Stanley's psychiatrists make no progress in his treatment. Boyle emphasizes the failure of psychoanalysis in Stanley's treatment by including flashback sections about his sexual history, including his humiliation by a Paris prostitute named Mireille Sancerre, his inability to consummate his marriage to Katherine, and his relationship with his domineering and emasculating mother. Stanley's ineffective Freudian psychiatrists cannot access these experiences in their sessions with their patient, resulting in the failure of their treatment. Boyle not only suggests psychiatry's ineffectiveness in treating patients but also the medical establishment's interest in not helping patients improve. All three of Stanley's doctors receive a handsome salary from Katherine for making sure that he stays sick and confined to Riven Rock.

In addition to being a critique of America's ineffective treatment of the mentally ill, *Riven Rock* is also a love story. As in *The Tortilla Curtain*, Boyle compares and contrasts the experiences and attitudes of two couples. In *Riven Rock* Stanley and Katherine McCormick are Boyle's first couple, and Eddie O'Kane and Giovannella Dimucci are his second. Because Stanley's illness prevents him from having a customary relationship with Katherine and confines him to Riven Rock, Boyle can test the limits of romantic love and loyalty. And Katherine, despite

Stanley's illness, his shortcomings as a husband, and his paranoid fear that she sleeps with other men when she is away from Riven Rock, remains loyal to her husband. She best demonstrates this loyalty in her continual hope that he will recover from his illness, her successful attempt to gain exclusive custody of him, and her efforts to find a cure for schizophrenia. Because of his illness, however, Stanley cannot reciprocate his wife's love in a conventional way, but he stays devoted to her throughout the novel in his own manner. In Stanley and Katherine's relationship, Boyle indicates the possibility of a steadfast romantic love, even if that love is a little crazy.

Boyle contrasts the McCormicks' relationship with Eddie and Giovannella's. Both Stanley and Eddie are confined to Riven Rock, the former as a patient and the latter as the head nurse, and both men are in relationships with independent women. But unlike Stanley, Eddie pursues women even as he makes sexist comments about them. Throughout the novel he criticizes Katherine for being an independent, smart, and wealthy woman, and yet he entertains sexual fantasies about her. He also behaves as a sexist and misogynist when he leaves his wife, Rosaleen, and their baby on the East Coast to work at Riven Rock. Eddie eventually begins a sexual relationship with Giovannella, whom Katherine characterizes as an Italian "peasant girl" (109). Eddie thinks of Giovannella: "He wanted to be naked. He wanted to be with her, wanted to touch her, taste her, run his fingers through her hair, over her breasts, into the wet silk of her cleft. He didn't write to Rosaleen" (105). The desire for and attainment of sexual contact inspires Eddie's relationship with Giovannella and other women. This sexual contact differentiates Eddie from Stanley, but Boyle's description of his uncontrollable sexual urges unites them. Both Eddie and Stanley are prisoners at Riven

Rock, the central difference being that the former has the freedom necessary to act on his sexual desires. The feminist Katherine recognizes Eddie's sexism and misogyny, asking him "Do you think a female is just an object, Mr. O'Kane, a bit of flesh put on this earth to satisfy your lusts?" and inspiring his animosity (110). Eddie cannot be loyal to the women in his life, and Boyle enunciates this disloyalty by constantly portraying Eddie's loyalty to his patient, Stanley. Eddie is another Boyle character who, like the father in "If the River Was Whiskey" and Truman Van Brunt in *World's End*, suffers from alcoholism and treats other characters badly as a result.

As a steadfast wife to Stanley and as an advocate for women's rights and a scientific cure for schizophrenia, Katherine is the hero of *Riven Rock*. In his 1998 interview with Laura Reynolds Adler, Boyle said, "To me, [Katherine] is really the center of the book, and becomes the hero of the book. Her story is pretty much heartbreaking."[35] When Boyle refers to Katherine as "the hero of the book," he points out the tragedy of her never being able to have a fulfilling relationship with the man she loves, despite her beauty, intelligence, sophistication, and passionate commitment to the pursuit of social justice. Even Eddie, who criticizes Katherine for being frigid and domineering, cannot negatively affect the reader's opinion of her. As Boyle's first genuinely admirable hero, Katherine marks a significant change in his art, a movement toward earnestness and sympathy.

CHAPTER 5

T. C. Boyle's Novels of the 2000s
A Friend of the Earth, Drop City, The Inner Circle, and Talk Talk

Boyle's four novels of the 2000s, *A Friend of the Earth*, *Drop City*, *The Inner Circle*, and *Talk Talk*, demonstrate his experimentalism as a writer, which he employs to write about controversial social issues. Published in 2000, *A Friend of the Earth* is an innovative, apocalyptic science-fiction novel that explores the dangerous impact of global warming on the environment and the role of radical environmentalist groups in protesting the companies that destroy the environment in their pursuit of capitalist gain. Boyle's novel of 2003, *Drop City*, moves away from science fiction and experiments with realism in its presentation of a group of hippies' attempt to establish a commune in the Alaskan wilderness. *The Inner Circle* of 2004 fictionalizes the life of Dr. Alfred Kinsey, the famous sex researcher of the Institute for Research in Sex, Gender, and Reproduction at Indiana University. Finally, Boyle's 2006 novel, *Talk Talk*, is a postmodern detective story and an exercise in metafiction that comments on identity theft and the experience of being blind in twenty-first-century America.

A Friend of the Earth (2000)

Boyle discussed the origin of *A Friend of the Earth*, his adventurous eighth novel, in his 2003 interview with Robert Birnbaum:

> All the books are allied in one way or another. . . . [*The*]
> *Tortilla Curtain* . . . is about illegal immigration on the sur-
> face but the subtext is about the environment and our over-
> population and our being animals in nature and how do we
> deal with all this? Then I did that full blown in . . . *A Friend
> of the Earth*, which is set in 2025. I'm extrapolating from
> everything that happens today. Well, if it's all true, global
> warming . . . then what will come if it?[1]

A Friend of the Earth is at once an important environmentalist
novel on the dangers of global warming, an experimental text
that employs both the conventions of realism and dystopian
science fiction, and a meditation on human love and relationships.[2] Its protagonist, Tyrone (Ty) O'Shaughnessy Tierwater, is
seventy-five years old in the year 2025. He, like Delaney Mossbacher in *The Tortilla Curtain*, is an environmentalist who
comes from a wealthy background. Unlike Delaney, however, Ty
gives most of his money, which comes from his father's shop-
ping-mall fortune, to a radical environmentalist organization,
Earth Forever! (an organization that, according to a 2000 interview about *A Friend of the Earth* with Gregory Daurer, Boyle
based on Earth First!), and participates and occasionally gets
arrested in its protests. Boyle narrates Ty's exploits in Earth Forever! in the third-person sections of the novel that cover the
years 1989 through 1997, whereas he chronicles Ty's current
adventures in the first-person sections of the novel that encom-
pass the years 2025 and 2026. Boyle employs this disjointed
temporal structure to write one of his most politically engaged
and emotionally moving novels.

On the surface Ty Tierwater seems to be just another of
Boyle's idealistic characters who lose the ability to love other
people as a result of the irrational pursuit of an obsession. But

Boyle differentiates Ty from these characters by writing *A Friend of the Earth* as an emotional exploration of the way in which Ty's quest for his obsession affects his relationship with his second wife, Andrea, and his daughter, Sierra.

In a flashback to the year 1989 that begins the novel, Ty is a willing member of Earth Forever!, who, along with Andrea, a thirteen-year-old Sierra, and their friend, Teo Van Sparks, protests the deforestation activities of a lumber company in the Siskiyou National Forest in Oregon by cementing himself to the ground in front of a grove of trees that is scheduled to be cut down. This demonstration becomes a disaster when the lumberjacks intimidate the protestors and "Sheriff Bob Hicks of Josephine County . . . handcuffed the four of them—even Sierra—and his deputies had a good laugh ripping the watchcaps off their heads, wadding them up and flinging them into the creek" (45). This disrespectful treatment enrages Ty, especially because of its effect on Sierra, as does his awareness that "there wasn't a single reporter on hand to bear witness" (46). As the novel progresses, Ty becomes very angry with the lumber companies and the government for the way in which they damage and ignore the environment, and he is increasingly dissatisfied with what he perceives to be Earth Forever!'s ineffective protests. This feeling of anger and dissatisfaction intensifies at various points in the novel, and then Ty behaves irrationally, obsessively, and violently. When the court decides that Sierra should live with foster parents after the Siskiyou protest, for example, Ty and an unwilling Andrea illegally retrieve her from her new home. When Ty is upset at the lumber companies and government for "forcing" him to live in seclusion after he and Andrea take Sierra from her foster home, he sets fire to a grove of trees that the Cross Creek Timber Company plants in the Sierra Nevada

Mountains to grow for timber. He eventually goes to jail twice in the novel, once for assaulting Sierra's foster father and brother and taking her away from them and again for attempting to sabotage several new General Electric power stanchions. These and other irrational actions in the novel, which Earth Forever! does not endorse, stem from Ty's personal anger just as much as they reflect his environmentalism.

Boyle suggests that political radicalism becomes ineffective and meaningless when individual activists lose their sense of rational objectivity and take corporate and government policies personally. While the reader is disappointed with Ty for losing his sense of detachment, he or she also forgives him because his lack of objectivity derives not only from his personal anger but also from his love for Andrea and Sierra. This love humanizes Ty, granting him depth as a character, and Boyle's exploration of it makes *A Friend of the Earth* an emotional meditation on the ways in which personal obsessions negatively affect relationships.

Ty's obsession damages his relationship with Andrea and Sierra because it deprives them of his company when he goes to jail for his crimes. This damage manifests itself most specifically in his relationship with Andrea when he asks her if she and Teo ever had sex before he married her: "All those nights on the road, Connecticut, New Jersey, wherever. You slept with him, didn't you?" (180). Ty fixates on this question throughout the novel, and he eventually wrongly accuses Andrea of having sex with Teo and other men: "How many guys did you fuck while I was in [prison]?" (303). This accusation, which makes him feel "low . . . like a toad, a criminal, a homewrecker" (303), occurs in the same conversation in which he indicates his dissatisfaction with the effectiveness of Earth Forever!, and it shows the extent to which his environmentalism and jealousy stem from a similar obsessive source. After Ty falsely accuses Andrea, she gives him a "look [that] had no reserve of love in it, not the smallest portion. She was beyond exasperation, beyond contempt even" (303). The reader empathizes with Ty in this moment, realizing that his accusation, even as it condemns him to years of separation from his wife, reveals his love—a love that he has difficulty expressing, even to himself. Ty's tragedy is that his anger and jealousy prevent him from admitting his inability to declare his love. But the sections of the novel set in the years 2025 and 2026 suggest that Ty eventually repents for his jealousy and anger and learns to be grateful for Andrea's company when they reunite during the environmental destruction of the future.

Ty's environmental fanaticism harms his relationship with Sierra: it causes her to be placed in a foster home; it isolates her from society and her peers when the Tierwater family lives in seclusion in the Sierra Mountains; and it leads to her death when she falls from a tall redwood tree that the Coast Lumber threatens to cut down for timber and in which she has lived for three years to prevent this from happening. Boyle describes Sierra's visits to Ty when he is in jail: "And his daughter—to her eyes, and hers alone, he was still a hero—tried to come when she could, but she was in college now, and she had papers to write, exams to take, rallies to attend, protests to organize, animals to liberate" (315). Sierra continues the family tradition of environmentalist activism, only she does not share Ty's anger, which largely derives from his feelings about the ways in which the lumber companies and government persecute her. Ty opposes Sierra's decision to live in the tree, but she rejects his authority, and Boyle's description of her fatal fall is one of the saddest passages in all his work: "But then the larger form came down—

much larger, a dark, streaking ball so huge and imminent the sky could never have contained it. There was a sound—sudden, roaring, wet—and then the forest was silent" (336). Boyle's rendering of Ty's attempt to convince Sierra to come down from the tree shortly before her death adds a sense of pathos to the conclusion of *A Friend of the Earth* that is missing from some of his earlier texts: "I was trying to tell my daughter . . . it was time to come down. Time to get on with life. Go to graduate school, get married, have children" (335).

Boyle's depiction of the ways in which environmental activism draws Ty away from his family and leads to Sierra's death seems to condemn and question the effectiveness of grassroots movements such as Earth Forever! and environmentalist activism in general. This might be the case if *A Friend of the Earth* only consisted of the late twentieth-century narrative. But Boyle includes the narrative of the years 2025 and 2026, which Ty himself narrates in the first person, to indicate that Ty, Andrea, Teo, Sierra, and the other members of Earth Forever! are correct in their assessment of the environment. In 2025 and 2026 the biosphere has collapsed, and many of the world's animals are extinct. Ty says, "It's not even the rainy season—or what we used to qualify as the rainy season, as if we knew anything about it in the first place—but the storms are stacked up out over the Pacific like pool balls on a billiard table and not a pocket in sight" (2). Ty goes on to categorize the new California weather as "floods, winds, thunder and lightening, even hail" (2) and describes a world in which environmental neglect has resulted in global destruction. As Joe Knowles notes in his review of the novel, "The metropolises of Helsinki and 'Greater Nome' now dwarf New York City. Brazil and New Zealand are desert countries."[3]

But Boyle does not narrate the twenty-first-century sections of the novel in the same manner as the late-twentieth-century sections. Instead he employs black comedy to satirize the environmental destruction that humanity creates for itself. The novel begins with a comic account of Ty, who now works as a caretaker of endangered animals on the Santa Ynez Valley estate of the aging millionaire pop star Maclovio (Mac) Pulchris, and his co-worker Chuy feeding a disgruntled hyena named Lily. Another section of the novel recounts Ty and Chuy's successful attempt to rescue three lions from drowning in a flood by housing them in the basement of Mac's mansion and the mayhem that ensues when the lions crawl up the dumbwaiter and kill Mac and some of his staff. In scenes such as this one, Boyle employs his characteristic method of suddenly switching from narrating a comic to a tragic event to disconcert the reader and make him or her react strongly to, in this case, the devastating impact of environmental neglect.

The aging of Ty's body parallels the destruction of the environment. The seventy-five-year-old Ty suffers from many physical ailments in the novel, including difficulties urinating and defecating. As Ty futilely tries to save his and Mac's animals and the people gathered at the estate, he embodies the decline of the environment.

Boyle's bleak comments at the Web site *Failbetter* on his contemporaneous short story, "After the Plague," exemplify the sense of hopelessness that pervades *A Friend of the Earth*, in which Ty's radical environmentalism and the more conventional tactics of Earth Forever! do not positively impact the status of the environment:

> We are all imminently doomed. That's all we know, the central and telling fact of our existence. Forget God. Forget

purpose. Forget dignity or even sense. It is over. And if our personal extinction weren't enough, there is always the really crucial knowledge that the sun will shortly (in three billion years or so) go to red giant phase and fry everything here (if the comet doesn't wipe us out first). So, what I'm saying is: what is exactly the point of being here in the first place?[4]

Boyle answers this question in "After the Plague" by indicating the ways in which Halloran, the short story's chief character, perpetuates his ethical hollowness, personal power, and selfishness after the plague destroys most of humanity. At the conclusion of *A Friend of the Earth*, Boyle places Ty in a situation similar to Halloran's. Even though the destruction of the biosphere in *A Friend of the Earth* does not lead to the immediate destruction of humanity, Ty, like Halloran, lives in seclusion with a woman. At the end of the novel, Ty and Andrea retreat to the same mountain cabin where they lived with Sierra after they abducted her from her foster parents. Walking near the cabin one day, they encounter a teenage girl who resembles Sierra when she was in her gothic phase: "That's when the girl appears, dressed all in black, a slight hunch to her shoulders, the long stride, high-laced black boots and hair the color of midnight in a cave" (349). When the girl asks them to identify the breed of dog of Petunia, the Tierwaters' leashed Patagonian fox, Ty responds by saying, "That's right . . . she's a dog. . . . And I'm a human being" (349). Elisabeth Schäfer-Wünsche reads this encounter, which concludes the novel, as satiric.[5] By not correcting the Sierra figure's identification of Petunia or giving her an account of his attempt to save the species, Ty decides to preserve her environmental ignorance. This decision may prevent her from needlessly dying for the cause like Sierra, but it also indicates the futility of environmental activism and illustrates Boyle's gloomy point that, despite all our efforts, "We are all imminently doomed." The only consolation that Boyle offers, as he does in *Budding Prospects*, *World's End*, and *The Road to Wellville*, is heterosexual monogamy as a temporary respite from the doom that awaits us all.

In a 2000 interview with Gregory Daurer, Boyle reaffirmed his position that no hope exists for the survival of humanity: "And this is an informed opinion because, by the way, I've read all the environmental tracts. And boy, that's why the public doesn't want to know about it, because it is so bleak. I can't find any hope in anything anybody's writing about the environment."[6] But despite Boyle's prognosis, *A Friend of the Earth* still serves as a screed against the dangers of global warming. As he told Alan Gottlieb in a 2000 interview, "I believe in being an environmentalist, in trying to preserve the other species. But I'm also kind of hopeless as well. I think it doesn't matter anymore."[7]

Drop City (2003)

In a 2003 interview Boyle spoke to Robert Birnbaum about *Drop City*, his ninth novel and a finalist for the National Book Award that year: "This is my first non-comic book. . . . And there are some comic scenes, but essentially it's played as realism and it's not the kind of satiric tone that I would usually bring to a work like this. Just to do something different and see if I can do it."[8] Not only a significant departure from Boyle's usual comic method, *Drop City* also marks his adoption of a realistic narrative style that strongly differs from the experimentation of his earlier novels.[9] Boyle's movement toward conventional realism makes *Drop City* one of his most accessible and entertaining novels and allows him to approach hippie idealism from a new angle. In *World's End*, *The Tortilla Curtain*, and *A Friend of the Earth*, Boyle pits hippie idealism in the form of environmentalism against a capitalist establishment. At the end of *World's End* and *A Friend of the Earth*, heterosexual hippie couples do not defeat the establishment with their ideals; rather, they choose to either work for change from within the system (Tom and Jessica in *World's End*) or completely exile themselves from the system (Ty and Andrea in *A Friend of the Earth*). In both novels Boyle argues that the capitalist establishment is more powerful than society's idealistic rebels. *Drop City* departs from these previous novels because it explores the hippie movement from within, finding a commonality between it and, as Boyle told C. P. Farley in an interview, the back-to-the-earth movement of the 1970s.[10]

Because Boyle writes *Drop City* as a realistic novel, he observes the realist conventions of setting, plot, and character. The novel takes place in 1970, a time of social unrest in America in which many college-aged Americans protested their country's involvement in the Vietnam conflict, participated in the civil rights movement, and advocated for the environment and an end to nuclear proliferation. These social concerns, along with rock music and experimentation with marijuana, psychedelic drugs such as LSD, free love, long hair, and bell-bottoms, were central to the hippie movement. During this period many hippies dropped out of mainstream American society and formed communes where they could pursue their ideals. Led by Norm Sender, a good-natured but ultimately selfish hippie whose wire-rimmed glasses, stoner speech, and paunch recall the Grateful

Dead's leader, Jerry Garcia (Norm and the other members of the commune pose as the Grateful Dead when they cross the border from Washington into Canada later in the novel), Boyle's Drop City, which is located in Sonoma, California, before it moves to a site on the Thirtymile River just outside Boynton, Alaska, is one of these communes.

Boyle constructs the plot of *Drop City* using the same comparative plotting technique that he features in many of his previous novels. The first plot line concerns the adventures of the hippies who live at Norm's Drop City commune. Over the course of the first half of the novel, the hippies of the commune suffer the persecution of the California authorities, who eventually force them to leave their land and, in a parody of the travels of the Joad clan in *The Grapes of Wrath* and Ken Kesey's Merry Pranksters in Tom Wolfe's *The Electric Kool-Aid Acid Test*, establish a new commune on land previously owned by Norm's uncle Roy on the Thirtymile River near Boynton, Alaska. The Alaskan section of the book, which occupies its second half, relates the naive hippies' travails and tests their commitment to the ideal of brotherhood as they try to work together to survive the brutal cold of an Alaskan winter.

The second plot line chronicles the romance and marriage of Cecil (Sess) and Pamela Harder. A former office worker from Anchorage who exemplifies the back-to-the-earth movement in her desire to live more purely in the wilderness of Alaska, Pamela marries Sess, a fur trapper who lives in a cabin on the Thirtymile River. Sess's hatred for a violent, hard-drinking, and dangerous ex-marine bush pilot named Joe Bosky, who continuously persecutes him, complicates their relationship. The hippie and Harder narratives intersect in the second half of the novel, when the hippies build their commune near the Harder cabin and Sess and Pamela befriend Boyle's two hippie heroes and residents of Drop City, Paulette (Star) Starr and Marco Connell.

Boyle's five main characters—Sess, Pamela, Star, Marco, and another hippie resident of Drop City named Ronnie (Pan) Sommers—drive the action of *Drop City*. Boyle writes the novel from the perspectives of these five characters and, except for Pan, sympathizes with them. Sess is a hard-working denizen of the Alaskan wilderness who respects tradition, the environment, and his new wife, Pamela. Whether hunting and fishing to stock his and Pamela's food cache in preparation for the upcoming long Alaskan winter or traveling upriver to Boynton to procure supplies, Sess is a tireless worker. Boyle also characterizes Sess as a traditionalist who follows the example of his mentor, Roy Sender. When Sess takes Marco fur trapping late in the novel, he teaches him Roy's practice of leaving a pot of frozen moose stew on the floor of the cabins in preparation for the next visit: "Roy taught me that. . . . Now I'm teaching you" (422). In addition to this respect for tradition, Sess respects the environment. On the same fur trapping expedition in which Sess passes on Roy's moose stew tradition, he and Marco discover a coyote in one of the traps. Sess expresses his sadness at this occurrence and his reverence for the environment: "Sess let out a low curse—it wasn't a wolf, but a coyote, all but worthless for its fur because no wrapped-up pampered matron on Park Avenue or Lake Shore Drive wanted to walk into a restaurant in a thing like that" (426). Sess, moreover, respects Pamela as an equal partner in his life in the wilderness. Even though the two divide their labor according to traditional gender roles—Sess hunts, fishes, and works the traps, while Pamela cooks and keeps up the cabin—they work together on many tasks, such as choosing new dogs after Joe Bosky kills their team.

Boyle makes Sess into a well-rounded character by emphasizing two traits in addition to his work ethic and respect for tradition, the environment, and his wife. First, Boyle characterizes Sess as a romantic who is hopelessly in love with Pamela and unsure of his prospects of marrying her. Sess best exemplifies his romanticism when he follows Pamela to the cabin of Howard Walpole, another Alaskan who hopes to marry her. Pamela agrees to spend time with the boring and sexually perverse Howard after she lives with Sess for a few days in his cabin. In a funny scene, the obsessed Sess stalks Pamela to Howard's house:

> Fifty yards out, he eased into a clot of highbush cran-berry and raised the binoculars to his eyes, and he didn't feel low or cheap at all. He didn't feel like a hopeless, sick-at-heart, unmanly, voyeuristic *creep*. Not him. No, he felt more like—well, a commando, that was it. A commando on a secret vital mission essential to the well-being of the entire country, not to mention a very specific plot of painstakingly husbanded bush at the mouth of the Thirtymile. (103)

Sess's humorous demonstration of his romanticism and his fear of appearing unmasculine, even to himself, humanizes him as a character and makes him instantly memorable.

Sess's hatred of Joe Bosky also lends him realism as a character. Caused by a dispute over Bosky's right to trap fur on Sess's property, this hatred escalates and becomes more irrational as the novel progresses. Bosky inspires Sess's anger at various points in the novel: he makes sexist comments to Pamela in a bar in Boynton; he tries to disrupt Sess and Pamela's wedding by aggressively dancing with Pamela's sister; he murders Sess's dogs;

and eventually he dies attempting to shoot Sess, Marco, and their team of dogs, whom he mistakes for a pack of wolves, from his plane. Despite Pamela's admonitions, Sess always responds to Bosky's violence, most memorably when he steals Bosky's prized 1965 Shelby Mustang, drives it to Fairbanks, and destroys it. Interestingly Boyle does not explain the origin of Bosky's animosity, which inspires Sess's angry retaliation. The reader knows only that Bosky is a former marine with a bad drinking problem who, as a poacher of wolf fur, seller of alcohol and drugs to Inuit people, and abuser of women, does not share Sess's reverence for the environment, respect for women, and observance of tradition. Regardless of Boyle's unsophisticated presentation of the motivations of the novel's chief villain, he creates Bosky to bring out Sess's hatred and, in so doing, lends Sess great humanity as a character.

Pamela also emerges as a well-rounded character. Unlike the hippies of Drop City who do not truly understand the hardships and hard work that await them in Alaska, Pamela understands what it means to live in the Alaskan wilderness during the harsh winter months. Like Sess, Pamela is a hard worker. Early in the novel Sess tells Pamela about Jill, a former girlfriend who attempted to live with him in his cabin through the winter. Unable to take the isolation of being shut up in the cabin during the long, dark winter months, Jill eventually broke down, and as Sess tells Pamela, she "went out there where we'd cleared all the trees and she stomped these huge letters in the snow . . . You know what they read—from the air, that is? JILL WANTS OUT" (94). Unlike Jill, Pamela can survive in the cabin and takes pleasure in such simple activities as "staring out into the moon-lit yard" from her window in the cabin, looking at animals (402).

In addition to being a hard worker and nature lover, Pamela is open minded and sexually monogamous. First, in befriending Star and other Drop City hippie women, Pamela experiments with drugs, smoking marijuana with them when they visit her in her cabin. Pamela is independently willing to engage in an activity of which her husband may not approve. She is so open minded that at the end of the novel she appears at the Drop City Christmas party "wearing the beaded hippie headband Star had given her" and ready to smoke "the joint that had just appeared magically in [Star's] hand" (438). Always a proponent of hetero-sexual monogamy, Boyle characterizes Pamela as being sexually monogamous in her marriage to Sess. This monogamy, which parallels the nature of Star's relationship with Marco, most obviously demonstrates itself in the fact that Pamela is a virgin on her and Sess's wedding night. In addition Pamela, like Star and many of Boyle's other female protagonists, enjoys the sex that she and her monogamous partner share: "She was a married woman . . . and she could indulge her wildest fantasies, do anything she wanted—stroke him, suck him" (117).

Marco, Boyle's third protagonist, represents a moderate form of the hippie ideal. First, Marco, like Sess and Pamela, practices sexual monogamy. When the hippie Lydia returns to Drop City after dancing in a strip club to earn money and contracting crabs there, she spreads the sexually transmitted disease among her friends. Marco tells Sess that Lydia "brought [the residents of Drop City] a little present from Fairbanks" and that he and Star do not have crabs: "I don't have them . . . And neither does Star. So that says something right there" (423). When Sess tells Marco, "Oh, you're hooked, brother, you're hooked. Your wandering days are over, all she wrote" (423), Boyle provides another endorsement of sexual monogamy.

Marco is independent—a trait that he shares with Sess. Star first meets Marco when he invites her to visit him in his treehouse: "Marco had built the treehouse from scrap lumber in a single afternoon . . . and when he reached down a bare arm to her she took hold of his hand and he pulled her up onto the branch alongside him as if she weighed no more than the circumambient air" (13). Like Sess, who becomes his mentor and father-figure later in the novel, Marco is self-sufficient enough to build his own shelter. This shelter, which he builds on the Drop City ranch in California, allows him independence even as he experiments in communal living. Marco also has a strong work ethic, which he demonstrates later in the novel when he is one of the leaders in the construction of the cabins at Drop City's new site in Alaska. Marco also indicates his independence through his interest in reading and in social justice. When Franklin, Lester, and other Drop City residents get angry at Marco for asking them to vacate the commune after they rape a fourteen-year-old girl, they scatter his books on the ground under his treehouse. Marco's interest in social justice also surfaces in his decision to dodge the Vietnam draft and in his favorite books, which include Steinbeck's *Of Mice and Men* and *Tortilla Flat*: two works by one of Boyle's favorite socially engaged writers.

Marco also parallels Sess in his willingness to learn and observe the traditional practices and values of the Alaskan wilderness. Unlike many of the novel's hippies, Marco shows that he respects the environment through his friendship with Sess, who teaches him how to make moose stew, leave a frozen pot of it on the floor of the cabin in preparation for the next visit, and set and remove animals from traps. In teaching Marco the fine points of surviving the winter in the Alaskan wilderness, Sess becomes a father-figure to him. When one remembers the failed father-son relationships in such novels and stories as *World's*

End, "If the River Was Whiskey," *East Is East*, and *The Road to Wellville*, one understands that the Sess-Marco relationship functions as possibly the first successful father-son relationship in all Boyle's fiction.

Like Marco, Star practices a moderate form of the hippie ideal, and as usual for Boyle, her sexually monogamous relationship with her boyfriend is instrumental to this ideal. A former schoolteacher, Star does have sex with her ex-boyfriend Pan at one point in the novel, but Boyle indicates that this break in fidelity is not a habit for Star, as it is for most of the other residents of Drop City. Boyle introduces Star in the first pages of the novel in the context of sexual monogamy when she recalls an experience that she and Pan had on their way to California from their hometown of Peterskill, New York. He describes the way in which Pan pressures her into having group sex with him and a nameless and mysterious "teepee cat": "You don't want to be an uptight bourgeois cunt like your mother, do you? . . . Or *my* mother, for shitsake? Come on, it's just the human body, it's natural—I mean, what is this?" (7). This incident, which shows the ways in which the hippie ideals of political rebellion and free love can be manipulated to harmful ends, is one of the main reasons why Star ends her affair with Pan and begins a sexually monogamous relationship with Marco. Star reinforces the connection between monogamy and gender roles when she and Pamela wait for Marco and Sess to return from their fur-trapping trip. Star and Pamela fulfill the traditional female roles of gossiping and keeping the cabin warm and the food hot while they wait for their men to return, even if they smoke a little pot to pass the time.

In addition to having a monogamous relationship with Marco, Star pursues issues of social justice and animal rights. Like Marco, she is outraged by the rape of the fourteen-year-old girl and joins her boyfriend in his efforts to have the alleged rapists vacate Drop City. Star demonstrates her concern for the commune's animals when she makes sure that the goats and dogs make the trip from California to Alaska. In Alaska a wolverine sneaks into the goat pen and kills the goats and the dog, Frodo. The deaths of the animals sadden Star, so much so that she refuses to let Norm and other Drop City residents use the meat of the goats for food. Star buries the animals as Marco watches: "Sweating till her eyes stung and the ends of her hair clung like tentacles at her throat, she dragged the carcasses of the goats—of Amanda and Dewlap, and yes, she could tell them apart now, even at this late hour when it no longer mattered and their eyes were closed to the world—dragged them across the yard and buried them" (305).

Whereas Sess, Pamela, Marco, and Star illustrate the ideals of hard work, self-sufficiency, tradition, monogamous sex, and reverence for the environment and animal life, Pan opposes these ideals. His opposition derives from his inauthenticity as a person. Like the rebels of "Greasy Lake" and Walter Van Brunt, who constructs himself as an existentialist rebel in *World's End*, Ronnie Sommers self-consciously constructs himself as "Pan," the Greek god of intoxication and revelry. This construction begins at a Peterskill Halloween party in which he dresses up as the Greek god, wearing "a pair of leftover devil's horns painted forest brown, pipes he'd found under a pile of crap in the music room in their old high school and the hairy-hocked leggings his mother had made for him on the sewing machine" (366). "That was the night," Boyle writes, "he'd left Ronnie behind, the night he'd *become* Pan for good" (366). Pan is an inauthentic construct though, and his hippie ideals derive more from his selfish needs than from any deeply held philosophy.

A prime example of Pan's selfishness is his lack of interest in social justice and unwillingness to work hard and be self-sufficient. When Pan witnesses the rape of the fourteen-year-old girl, he does nothing to intervene and, the text implies, may have joined in. In any case he does not align himself with Marco and Star when they demand that Lester, Franklin, and the other rapists leave Drop City. In addition Pan does not display the work ethic of Sess, Pamela, Marco, and Star. He does not help Marco and some of the other residents when they design and build the cabins at the new Drop City site in Alaska. Instead Pan travels to Boynton with money that the residents give him to purchase supplies. When Pan returns to Drop City in Joe Bosky's plane, the residents find out that he has used their money to purchase marijuana, which he in turn tries to sell to them. At a communal meal, Pan tells residents that the marijuana is "an investment for all of [them]," and Mendocino Bill retorts, "Yeah, right . . . you mean the pot you tried to sell me this morning for thirty bucks a lid?" (328). Pan's attempt to sell marijuana to his friends indicates his desire to exploit them for monetary profit as well as his unwillingness to work hard and be self-sufficient at Drop City. He also reveals his exploitative nature and lack of self-sufficiency when he steals the commune's rifles and money from Star's backpack.

Like other less attractive Boyle characters such as Walter Van Brunt in *World's End*, Ruth Dershowitz in *East Is East*, and Eddie O'Kane in *Riven Rock*, Pan is sexually promiscuous. In fact Pan continually uses the hippie ideal of free love to justify his attempt to fulfill his sexual desires. The best example of Pan's sexual promiscuity occurs when he contracts crabs from Lydia, whom he does not respect and uses to gratify his sexual urges.

Pan also makes the mistake of choosing Joe Bosky as his father-figure and mentor. Boyle structures the final chapters of *Drop City* to allow the reader to contrast Pan's relationship with Bosky to Marco's relationship with Sess. Whereas Sess teaches Marco to revere nature through the observance of tradition, Bosky teaches Pan to exploit both the environment through the illegal procurement of wolf hides and the native peoples by selling them alcohol and drugs. Bosky's example is ultimately fatal for both the teacher and the student when he crashes their plane while attempting to shoot Sess, Marco, and their team of dogs. After the crash Pan develops a plan to save the seriously injured Bosky and himself. He builds a fire and then thinks, "What he would do was wait for morning, for the half-life and the glow painted round the hills to the south—that would give him direction, and he'd work his way east to the river and then go north for Drop City" (418). This elaborate plan, like the similarly elaborate plan of the protagonist in Jack London's naturalist story "To Build a Fire," fails when Pan makes the mistake of trying to satisfy his craving for alcohol by drinking the dangerously and ultimately fatally cold contents of his whiskey flask. Pan dies, another example of a Boyle character who does not understand the dangerous power of nature. Like Walter Van Brunt in *World's End*, Pan follows an alcoholic father-figure with an obsessive personality and suffers because of it. As in other Boyle texts such as *World's End*, "If the River Was Whiskey," and "Up against the Wall," the abuse of alcohol in *Drop City* leads to destruction.

The emergence of Joe Bosky as the novel's central villain indicates a lack of political engagement in Boyle's consideration of the origin of evil in *Drop City*. As Dwight Garner points out in his *New York Times* review of *Drop City*, "Boyle makes some mistakes. He gives us an Alaskan bad guy, a half-cocked former marine named Joe Bosky, who is so one-dimensional he might as well be named Sergeant Evil."[11] Bosky's evil deeds, which include his alcoholism, sexism, and exploitation of the environment and other people, come from his own corrupt nature and not from his exposure to authoritarian values in Vietnam. In *Drop City*, evil results from individual natures and not social institutions. This is a surprisingly unsophisticated presentation of evil in which individual characters and not social systems cause harm, and because of this, Boyle cannot take his usual strong stand against sexism, racism, and the exploitation and destruction of the environment. Nonetheless the novel's realism signifies a new development in Boyle's art.

The Inner Circle (2004)

Published just a year after *Drop City*, Boyle's tenth novel, *The Inner Circle*, returns to the familiar territory of satirizing the life, career, and philosophy of a famous historical American idealist, scientist, and authoritarian.[12] In this regard Boyle's novel about the life of Dr. Alfred Kinsey (who was known as "Prok" to his family, friends, and colleagues), the famous American entomologist, sex researcher, and author of two books, *Sexual Behavior in the Human Male* (1948) and *Sexual Behavior in the Human Female* (1953), that helped spark the sexual revolution in America in the 1960s, resembles his lampooning of Mungo Park in *Water Music*, Dr. John Harvey Kellogg in *The Road to Wellville*, and Stanley McCormick's psychiatrists in *Riven Rock*. But this is only a surface resemblance because Boyle in *The Inner Circle*, for the most part, abandons his previous method of satirizing his victims in scenes of antic and grotesque comedy and focuses instead on presenting Kinsey's life in a manner that recalls his work in *Drop City*, his self-proclaimed initial foray into realism. *The Inner Circle*, however, is not a realist text. Never interested in repeating previous methods, here Boyle ventures for the first time into modernism. *The Inner Circle* follows the example of modernist texts as an exploration of the ways in which subjective perceptions influence the construction of narrative and, by extension, the formation of identity. This exploration allows Boyle to investigate American idealism, science, and authoritarianism in a new light.

The first sentence of *The Inner Circle* announces Boyle's interest in positioning his text in the modernist tradition. The novel begins, "Looking back on it now, I don't think I was ever actually 'sex shy' (to use one of Prok's pet phrases), but I'll admit I was pretty naïve when I first came to him, not to mention hopelessly dull and conventional" (3). The reader quickly learns that Boyle's narrator is John Milk, who, at the novel's opening in 1939, is a senior English major at Indiana University, an attendee of Kinsey's controversial "six unexpurgated lectures (with audiovisual aids) . . . on the physiology of intramarital relations" (6), and a future member of Kinsey's inner circle—that is, the team of sex researchers who help him collect the data he uses in his books and who work at his Institute for Research in Sex, Gender, and Reproduction at Indiana University. Boyle's first sentence sets up Milk as the first-person narrator of the novel and gives important insight into his personality. Milk's use of multiple clauses and the phrase "I'll admit" lends his remarks a tentative and careful tone that reveals the equally tentative and careful nature of his personality. When Milk describes how he spent his summer vacation at home in Michigan City "lonely, bored to tears, masturbating twice a day in [his] attic room that was like a sweatbox in a penal institution" and reading John

Donne, Andrew Marvell, and "Sir Philip Sidney's *Astrophel and Stella* three times in preparation for an English literature course [he] was looking forward to in the fall" (4), he employs the language of imprisonment to confess his punitive evaluation of his experience of sexual pleasure through masturbation and refers to Donne, Marvell, and Sidney to convey his literary and "metaphysical" way of understanding sexuality. Milk is a conservative and sexually imprisoned narrator to whom the messianic Kinsey offers the potential for sexual freedom. Moreover Milk's conservative and literary personality, as well as his desire to be sexually liberated by Kinsey, negatively affects the objective validity of his narrative of Kinsey's private and public sexual theories and practices. Milk is an unreliable narrator, a subjective observer, interpreter, and chronicler in the modernist tradition. Milk's text, accordingly, indicates much more about his subjective experience than any objective, factual reality.

Like many of Boyle's previous books, *The Inner Circle* features a protagonist whose father is dead. The intelligent, charismatic, and passionate Kinsey becomes a father-figure to Milk. Recalling Kinsey's offer to raise his salary to help him purchase a home for himself and his pregnant wife, Iris, Milk writes, "To think that he was looking out for me still, me, John Milk, nobody really, a former student, the least of his employees, and willing to sacrifice his own finances into the bargain—it was just too much. My father was dead, my mother remote. But Prok, Prok was there for me, anticipating my needs—our needs, Iris's and mine—as if I were his own flesh and blood" (304). Milk emphasizes the way in which he views Kinsey as a father who financially provides for his symbolic son. Milk also dreams of the familial role that he anticipates for Kinsey after the birth of his son: "I saw a succession of birthday parties stretching on over the years, balloons, flowers, the cutting of the cake. Prok lifting my son to his shoulders and parading round the room with him, uncle, godfather, mentor" (334). In addition Milk remembers Kinsey referring to him explicitly as his son: "But really, I do think that as my colleague, as my co-researcher— almost my son, John, my *son*—you have to realize that emotions, and emotional outbursts, have no place in our research" (403).

Kinsey's fatherly remarks on the desirability of maintaining a firm separation between science and emotion form the basis of his father-son conflict with Milk. This separation and resultant conflict derive from Kinsey's physiological and "objective" approach to sexuality, which neither accounts for the role of emotion in sex nor provides a sexual ethics. The best example of Kinsey's approach occurs when he hosts his final "musical evening" of the novel. During these musical evenings, which transpire repeatedly throughout the novel, Kinsey furnishes his guests with alcoholic drinks, plays a recording of and lectures on a piece of classical music, and then retires to his attic with his wife, Mac, and guests to engage in sexual experiments, including, at various times in the novel, group sex, masturbation, heterosexual and homosexual sex, and voyeurism. The final musical evening in the novel entails Kinsey, Mac, Milk, Iris, and the other members of Kinsey's inner circle and their wives having group sex and being filmed in the process. When Aspinall, Kinsey's staff filmmaker, begins filming with "the skirts of his trench coat drooping like wings so that he was like a big carrion bird hunkered over an object of supreme interest" (396), Milk refuses to be the first to be filmed having sex. Milk's refusal combines with the simile, which in comparing Aspinall to "a big carrion bird" lends the scene an atmosphere of death, destruction, and decay, to indicate his questioning of his symbolic father's "scientific methods." After Purvis Corcoran, an "exhibitionist" and member of Kinsey's inner circle (396), is filmed having sex with Kinsey and is followed by various couples from the group, the naked Kinsey attempts to pressure Milk and Iris into participating: "[Kinsey] was erect again, heavy in the gut, the cords of his knees and lower legs pulled taut over flesh that was tough as jerked meat. His head loomed. His face. 'Now, Milk,' he said, 'are you ready now? You and your own wife'" (397). Milk describes Kinsey as a large, sexually potent, and aging man who wields power over him—a veritable image of Freud's oedipal father. Iris responds to Kinsey's request by offering to have sex with Corcoran, but Kinsey expresses his own desire to have sex with Iris. When Kinsey tries to force the issue with the reluctant Iris, with Milk's narrative noting the physical and phallic prowess of Kinsey's "massive hardened arterial legs" (397), Milk tackles his adversary, leaving him "on his back in the middle of the floor" before running away with Iris in tow (397). Milk engages in a primal physical and violent battle with his symbolic father, and the guilt that he experiences afterward relates to "the sense of guilt [that] is an expression of the conflict due to ambivalence, of the external struggle between Eros and the instinct of destruction or death,"[13] which Freud describes in his remarks on the Oedipus complex in *Civilization and Its Discontents*. Milk's feeling of guilt after he tackles Kinsey in defense of his wife—feeling remorseful, he does not "go into work the next day" (398)—marks the ambivalence of the love-hate relationship that he shares with his symbolic father.

According to Freud the conflict with and symbolic murder of the father and the son's ensuing sense of guilt ultimately result in the establishment of conscience, the creation of the superego, and the foundation of civilization.[14] Using Freud's comment, the reader of *The Inner Circle* can understand Milk's battle with Kinsey as Boyle's way of exploring the role of sex in the formation of civilization. By pitting Milk and his defense of heterosexual monogamy against Kinsey and his science of emotionless heterosexual and homosexual "freedom," Boyle upholds the view that he first expressed in *Budding Prospects* of the primacy of heterosexual monogamy and romantic love in humanity's ability to experience a degree of freedom within the constraints of civilization. In defending heterosexual monogamy and romantic love, Milk feels the unease of his symbolic father's judgment and of his own guilty conscience, but this feeling forms the basis of a free moral civilization that exists in opposition to Kinsey's dictatorial reign over his inner circle.

In presenting Kinsey's tyrannical rule, Boyle returns to the critique of idealism, science, and authority that preoccupied him in earlier texts such as *Water Music*, *The Road to Wellville*, and *Riven Rock*. Like Mungo Park's final fatal voyage up the Niger River, Dr. John Harvey Kellogg's administration of the San and murder of his adoptive son, and the psychiatrists' mistreatment of Stanley McCormick, Kinsey's idealistic attempt to use science —in this case to liberate the members of his inner circle and, indeed, all Americans from sexual oppression—paradoxically leads to the establishment of himself as an authoritarian despot who harms those closest to him. Kinsey descends to a state of animality despite his proclamation of the primacy of objective scientific inquiry.

Milk's narrative captures Kinsey's authoritarianism through its presentation of the specific aspects of the inner circle's research for the *Sexual Behavior in the Human Male* and *Sexual Behavior in the Human Female* books. Kinsey's initial methodology includes surveying the sexual experiences of thousands of

Americans from all walks of life in personal interviews taken by members of the inner circle. To obtain the surveys, Kinsey and the members of his team travel to various cities and college campuses, where they expect to gather representative data of the sexual experiences of Americans. Milk recalls visiting "the homosexual underground in Indianapolis and Chicago, as well as at least one prison and the state work farm where Prok had made so many of his most valuable contacts" and traveling to Gary, Indiana, to gather "black histories" (125). On the trip to Gary, Milk interviews a prostitute, who tells him "what you might expect from a girl in her position—relations at puberty with both her father and an older brother, marriage at fourteen, the move north from Mississippi, abandonment, the pimp, the succession of johns and venereal diseases" (129). In describing this interview, Milk implicitly reveals several of the flaws in Kinsey's methodology and, by extension, his personality. First, Kinsey does not ask Milk in taking the survey and analyzing its results to formulate an ethical response to the social, political, and racial factors that lead to the prostitute's terrible sexual experiences and horrendous life. Kinsey's so-called objective methodology is a form of thought control that makes it impossible for Milk to question the authority behind American social structures. Just as Milk does not interrogate the social structures that determine the life of the prostitute, he also does not interrogate Kinsey's dictatorship of the inner circle. Second, Kinsey's methodology discloses the impossibility of maintaining ethical, emotional, and sexual objectivity:

> Unprofessionally, [Milk] wanted to get up from [his] chair and hug her and tell her it was all right, that things would get better, though [he] knew they wouldn't. Unprofessionally, [he] wanted to strip the clothes from her and have her

> there on the bed and watch her squirm beneath [him.] [He]
> didn't act on either impulse. [He] just closed down [his]
> mind and recorded her history, one of the thousands that
> would be fed into the pot. (129)

Milk's use of the word "unprofessionally" in these sentences
links the concept of professionalism to Kinsey's authority—that
is, according to Kinsey, it is unprofessional and incorrect for one
of his workers to have an ethical, emotional, and sexual response
to an interviewee. In Kinsey's view professionalism entails the
suppression of ethical, emotional, and sexual responses. Milk
suggests that Kinsey's methodology, which on the surface appears as a means of liberation from sexual oppression, is in actuality an authoritarian tactic that limits the freedom of both the
interviewer and the interviewee.

Kinsey himself exposes the hypocrisy of his methodology and
reveals himself as an authoritarian at various points in Milk's
narrative. The most obvious example of Kinsey's hypocrisy
occurs in the musical evenings. These evenings create an emotional tension in the group that makes methodological objectivity impossible. Kinsey's seduction of Milk early in the novel only
adds to this tension. After relating that Kinsey has discovered
that he has read his employer's sexual history without receiving
his permission to do so, Milk writes,

> And then something strange happened, the last thing I
> would have expected under the circumstances—he kissed
> me. Leaned in, closed his eyes and kissed me. Some period
> of time passed during which neither of us spoke, then he
> took me by the hand and led me up the stairs to the spare
> room in the attic, and I remember a Ping-Pong table there,
> children's things, a fishing rod, an old sewing machine—

and a bed. I didn't go home that night, not until very late.
(73–74)

Kinsey uses his position as Milk's boss, as well as his power to punish him, as a means of fulfilling his own sexual desire. He blurs the boundary between discipline and sex, all the while asserting his power over Milk and taking him to his attic, the site of his more controversial sexual adventures, which he wishes to keep hidden from the world. Milk's rendering of the details of the scene characterizes the sex between Kinsey as a father-figure and Milk as a son-figure as being almost incestuous in nature. These images of childhood also demonstrate the extent to which Kinsey corrupts Milk's innocence in the attic. In addition Milk's remembrance of the way in which Kinsey "closed his eyes" when he first kisses him implies that Kinsey himself experiences the very romantic emotions against which he thunders elsewhere in the book.

Other aspects of Kinsey's research include the watching of prostitutes having sex with men; the watching and filming of inner circle members having sex with each other, volunteers, and eventually their wives; and the filming of one thousand masturbating men in New York city to "study . . . the means of sperm emission in the human male" (355). The latter study provides insight into the authoritarianism of Kinsey's methodology. Wanting to reject the claim in the existing "medical literature . . . that it was necessary for sperm to spurt out under pressure in order for fertilization to occur" and find evidence for his own claim that "the majority of males did not spurt but rather dribbled" (355), Kinsey arranges to film the mass masturbation experiment. Kinsey, Aspinall, and the other members of the inner circle set up their camera in a hotel room and budget "five minutes per man, one after the other coming in, removing his clothes and taking his position on the floor even as the man before him vacated it, a kind of assembly line" (357). Milk's comparison of Kinsey's experiment to an assembly line indicates the way in which his methods dehumanize the participants in the study. When Kinsey realizes that the "subjects unable to perform for the camera, those who needed extra time, a trip to the bathroom and so on" cause "inevitable delays" (357), he commands one of the experiment's participants as follows: "If you could please just come now—" (358). In making this demand of the participant, Kinsey illustrates the extent to which his methodology and, by extension, he himself desire to exert control over natural processes and people.

Kinsey maintains a similar authority over the members of the inner circle in the initiation rituals in which they must participate before he hires them. When Kinsey interviews Oscar Rutledge for a position on his staff, he takes him to his attic, along with Milk, Corcoran, and a young woman named Betty. Then he, Milk, and Rutledge watch as Corcoran and Betty have sex. Milk graphically and scientifically describes the initiation: "Her hands became more animated, tugging his shirt, tearing loose the buttons, a kind of frenzy building till they were both naked and Corcoran was on his knees spreading her legs and performing cunnilingus on her while she snatched at his hair and ears and tugged as if she would pull him into her" (291). Both Milk and Rutledge struggle to keep their scientific objectivity as they watch, and Milk reports that "[he'd] never yet been so aroused in [his] life" and that Rutledge "was aroused—his trousers were tented in the crotch—and though he tried to be surreptitious about it, tried to remain focused and detached, he began to move his hands in his lap" (291). In addition to demonstrating the impossibility of upholding scientific objectivity in Kinsey's experiments, this scene is a further indication of Kinsey's authoritarian personality. Before the group goes to the attic, Kinsey "seemed preternaturally excited, like a boy on the eve of his birthday" (288). Milk's observation suggests the extent to which Kinsey functions not as a detached scientist but as an emotionally stunted man with the money and power to create situations that permit him and the members of his inner circle to realize their adolescent sexual fantasies. These situations serve as initiation rituals that test the applicant's willingness to observe Kinsey's authority and live in the fantasy world of which he is the master.

At the conclusion of the novel, Milk recalls the time when he and Corcoran arrived at the institute to unload Robert Latou Dickinson's "library, the histories he'd taken, his sex diaries and erotica collection," as well as his "models . . . of human genitalia, depicted in the act of coitus, in a scale of roughly five to one, so that the phallus is nearly a yard long and the clay vagina meant to receive it proportional in every way" (417). Kinsey, whose "very exacting advice as to routes, padding to protect the models, the ideal speed [they] should maintain, how much rest [they] should need and where [they] should stop for meals, et cetera" indicates further his authoritarian personality (418), offers to assist Milk with his unloading: "I can see that you don't know the first thing about unloading an automobile. Here . . . let me" (418). In responding to Kinsey's offer, which he records in the final paragraph of his narrative, Milk has the opportunity to reject the authority of the man who functions as his symbolic father and thereby overcome the guilt that he experiences after he tackles him in defense of Iris. Milk, however, does not take advantage of this opportunity, writing that he "feel[s] [Kinsey] take the load from [him] as if it had never been there at all"

(418). In the final sentence of the novel, which is importantly rendered in the present tense, Milk suggests that he willingly continues to give up his freedom and bow down before this authoritarian father-figure. Even though his narrative discloses Kinsey's tyrannical system, Milk states at the novel's conclusion that it is more psychically comforting for him to surrender his freedom to this system rather than to carry the "load" of thinking for himself.

Talk Talk (2006)

Published in 2006, *Talk Talk*,[15] Boyle's eleventh novel, departs significantly from the realism of *Drop City* and the modernism of *The Inner Circle*. As *A Friend of the Earth* does with regard to science fiction and dystopian fiction, *Talk Talk* appropriates the conventions of a specific form of genre fiction and employs them to serve its author's thematic purposes. While not as structurally, aesthetically, and thematically radical as its more experimental predecessors, *Talk Talk* adopts the strategies of the postmodern detective narrative to explore social issues, such as identity theft and the treatment of the deaf and disabled, that are not found in Boyle's previous novels. Despite having one of the weakest endings of all Boyle's works, *Talk Talk*, as an amalgamation of postmodern detective narratives and socially engaged narratives, signifies an important transformation of his art.

Michael Holquist has provided helpful insight into how postmodern detective fiction differs from traditional detective fiction. Traditional detective stories, such as those written by Edgar Allan Poe and Sir Arthur Conan Doyle, proclaim the power of human logic and reason to overcome mysteries. The author advances the plot by providing vital clues that the reader and detective both use to solve the mystery. The genre is firmly grounded in the world of human experience and allows no room at the end of the narrative for transcendent mysteries or existential uncertainty. In contrast postmodern detective fiction—or, as Holquist puts it, metaphysical detective fiction—subverts traditional detective narrative structures by placing greater emphasis on character, demonstrating the ultimate impossibility of using logic and reason to answer existential questions, and arguing for the existence of transcendent mysteries.[16]

Dana Halter and her boyfriend Bridger Martin, the two chief protagonists and detectives in *Talk Talk*, do not question transcendent mysteries. But this does not mean that Boyle does not subvert the traditional form of the detective novel. The subversion results from his awareness of the ways in which narrative structures—and especially those found in popular cinema and television—shape the ways in which people interpret the world. Bridger Martin works as a special effects technician for Digital Dynasty on "the last installment of a trilogy set on a distant and inimical planet where saurian warlords battled for dominance and human mercenaries shifted allegiance in observance of tenets of an ancient warrior code" (12). Bridger's job is to "superimpos[e] the three-dimensionally photographed face of the film's action hero, Kade (or *The* Kade, as he was now being billed), over the white helmet of a stuntman on a futuristic blade-sprouting chopper that shot up a ramp and off a cliff to skim one of Drex III's lakes of fire and propel its driver into the heart of the enemy camp where he would proceed to hack and gouge and face-kick one hapless lizard warrior after another" (13). By placing this description of Bridger's job at the beginning of the novel, Boyle provides the reader with an interpretive strategy to guide his or her reading of the rest of the book. Just as Bridger superimposes Kade's head over the stuntman's helmet, the reader superimposes Bridger's head over Kade's head and Dana's head over the head of the film's star actress, Lara Sikorsky. As they work as detectives to discover the name and location of Peck Wilson, the man who steals both their identities in the novel, Bridger and Dana become action heroes and engage in many of the violent activities and exciting adventures that characterize the lives of Kade and Lara.

The best example of the ways in which the story of Bridger and Dana duplicates the adventures of cinematic action heroes such as Kade and Lara occurs late in the novel, when they trace Peck to his mother's house in Peterskill, New York, and confront him. By aggressively approaching and accusing Peck and defending the rights of his girlfriend, Bridger plays the role of action hero. As is typical for a villain in a detective and adventure story, Peck knows the martial art of tae kwon do, which he uses to attack the unsuspecting and defenseless Bridger: "The first blow—the *sonnal mok anchigi*, knifehand strike to the neck—rocked him, and then two quick chops to drop his arms, ride back on the left foot and punch through the windpipe with the right" (278). After the duplicitous villain seriously injures his antagonist, he engages in another activity typical both to detective and adventure narratives: the chase of the heroine through the streets. Dana eludes Peck in this chase and eventually visits Bridger in the hospital, where she notices in a waiting room that "the TV on the wall . . . was tuned . . . to an overwrought drama about emergency room doctors" (294). Boyle refers to this TV drama and makes connections between Bridger, Dana, and Peck and the latest installment in Kade's trilogy to suggest that individuals understand both their personal experiences and narrative texts through their previous exposure to other narrative structures.

Boyle constructs a plot that both exposes the conventions of detective fiction and employs those conventions to tell an exciting story. The main plot centers around Dana, an intelligent and beautiful thirty-something deaf woman whose identity is stolen by William "Peck" Wilson, whom Boyle names after Edgar Allan Poe's identity thief, William Wilson. When Dana is arrested and incarcerated for a series of crimes that Peck commits, she earns the reader's sympathy as an innocent victim. She gains more of the reader's sympathy after she is released from prison and learns that Peck's crimes are not serious enough to warrant a sustained police investigation. Her boyfriend, Bridger, helps her in her quest to bring Peck, who also steals his identity, to justice. The two become detectives on this quest, eventually taking justice into their own hands, discovering Peck's true identity, and following him across the country from the San Roque area of California to his hometown of Peterskill. Boyle prevents this plot from falling into cliché by making metafictional references to Kade's trilogy and the TV hospital drama that plays as Dana waits for Bridger in the hospital waiting room, as well as by constructing Dana as a deaf woman and Peck as a gourmet chef.

The social criticism inherent in the challenges and travails Dana faces as a deaf woman add depth to Boyle's plot. In many of his previous novels, Boyle wrote about the suffering of the poor and socially marginalized, especially in his presentation of racial intolerance in *World's End*, *East Is East*, and *The Tortilla Curtain* and his depiction of the treatment of the mentally ill in *Riven Rock*. *Talk Talk* fits into the tradition of these novels by exposing the prejudice faced by deaf people, as well as their feelings of loneliness and alienation. Dana repeatedly faces prejudice in the novel. When she and Bridger begin their quest to find Peck, they stop at a Mexican restaurant to have lunch. When

Dana orders "the fifth item on the list, *tostada de pollo*" and indicates her choice by saying "as clearly as she could, 'Number Five, please,'" she understands that the woman behind the counter knows that she is deaf and treats her badly because of her disability (121). The woman does not serve Dana a tostada: "When their order came up, [Bridger] went to the counter and brought back a paper plate and set it before her. The dish it contained didn't look like a tostada. For one thing, there was no shell; for another, no lettuce. Instead, what she got seemed to be some kind of organ meat in gravy and a wash of melted cheese" (122). Realizing that the woman gives her this disgusting meal as a punishment for her deafness, Dana feels discriminated against and loses her appetite. Boyle explores the feelings of loneliness that experiences such as the one in the Mexican restaurant partially cause. When Dana and Bridger bump into one of Bridger's college friends and his wife in Lake Tahoe, where they have followed Peck, Dana cannot participate fully in their conversation, despite her excellent abilities as a lip reader: "Dana lost track of what they were saying. Eventually, she just lowered her eyes and concentrated on the plate before her" (203). But Boyle does not reference social prejudice and feelings of loneliness to construct Dana as a victim; rather, she triumphs over her disability by receiving her Ph.D., living on her own, and developing her lip-reading skills. In fact Boyle portrays many of the technologies that Dana uses to overcome her disability, including a phone that allows her to make calls as text messages and the light that flashes in her apartment as a doorbell, to emphasize the ways in which deaf people successfully integrate themselves into the hearing world and overcome their disabilities. This portrayal provides the hearing world with essential information about the lives of deaf people, information that humanizes them as individuals.

In addition to offering sympathetic and complex portrayals of deaf people, *Talk Talk* includes an elaborate depiction of identity theft from the perspectives of both the victim and the perpetrator. This depiction helps construct *Talk Talk* as a novel about a prevalent and controversial contemporary social issue. The opening section explores identity theft from the perspective of a victim, Dana, and chronicles her experiences from when she is arrested and goes to jail for the crimes committed by Peck to her eventual release from prison. Boyle describes Dana's anxieties about using the toilet in her jail cell, her cellmate Angela whose smell is "a savage working odor of the streets, of festering clothes, body secretions, food gone rancid" (30), her dinner of "two slices of white bread encasing a thin sliver of bologna with a dab of ketchup painted like a bull's-eye in the middle of it, spotted yellow apple, sugary fruit drink in a wax carton with malleable straw attached" (32), and her general fear, loneliness, and confusion at being wrongly arrested. Boyle refers to Dana's confinement and negative reaction to the prison food to contrast her experiences to Peck's, which at this point of the novel include freedom and the preparation and consumption of gourmet food.

Later in the novel Boyle presents identity theft from the perspective of the perpetrator, providing a veritable how-to guide for committing the crime, as well as a discussion of the ease with which the crime can occur in contemporary society. Peck learns the fine points of identity theft from his cellmate Sandman, whom he meets after being incarcerated for stealing the identity of his estranged wife, Gina, and her father, assaulting Gina's boyfriend, and "pour[ing] six plastic jugs of muriatic acid over the finish" of his car and "slash[ing] the tires and [taking] out the windshield for good measure" (135). Sandman teaches Peck his life's mantra, "Be anybody you can be," and the student follows his instructor's lesson when he gets out of prison and finds a "sheaf of discarded medical forms, replete with names, addresses, birth dates and social security numbers" in a dumpster outside a Peterskill medical building (164). Peck uses the forms to open a checking account and obtain credit cards in the name of one of the patients, eventually employing this and similar strategies to assume the identities of other people, including Dana and Bridger, and becoming rich in the process. Boyle's presentation of the facility with which Peck perpetrates his crimes alerts the reader to the possibility of identity theft occurring in his or her own life.

In presenting the motivation for Peck's crimes, however, Boyle runs into the same difficulties that hampered his characterization of Joe Bosky in *Drop City*. Boyle traces Peck's motivation in a series of episodes in which Peck reflects on his life. He remembers his marriage to Gina, his days working as a chef in an Italian restaurant called Fiorentino's, his extramarital affairs, the loss of the Italian restaurants he opens and runs with the financial assistance of his father-in-law after he and Gina get divorced, and his trip to jail for identity theft and assault. Peck's downfall originates in his inability to "take criticism well" (100): "No matter what, he was always right, even if he was wrong, and he could prove it with one jab of his right hand" (101). When Peck faces criticism and does not get his way, he reacts with anger and violence. In *Talk Talk*, therefore, evil arises from the character flaws of individuals and not from repressive political, social, and economic systems.

The unsatisfactory ending contributes to Boyle's unsophisticated presentation of evil in *Talk Talk*. In her *New York Times* review of the novel, Michiko Kakutani recognizes the unsuccessful nature of this ending: "[Dana, Bridger, and Peck's] story, told in chapters that alternate between each one's point of view, is funny, engaging and suspenseful, and sadly undermined by a forced, slap-dash ending that feels as if it had been grafted on at the last minute in a desperate effort to find some way of bringing this novel to a close."[17] The weak ending has other serious consequences for the book. At the end of the novel, Dana inexplicably lets Peck escape the authorities, and she and Bridger—also inexplicably—decide to end their relationship so that they can pursue their careers. While making a claim about her personal ability to overcome her anger toward Peck, Dana's decision not to bring him to justice distances her from Bridger, Frank Calabrese, Gina, Natalia, and other members of the community who suffer as a result of his crimes. The personal morality and redemption of an individual character is allowed to take precedence over justice in the greater social community. And by not continuing her relationship with Bridger, Dana favors her career over human relationships. Boyle may have intended this to be one of his usual tragic and unhappy endings, but this conclusion, unlike many of his previous conclusions, compromises the political and social effectiveness of the novel as a whole.

Notes

Chapter 1—Understanding T. C. Boyle

1. T. C. Boyle, "This Monkey, My Back," *TCBoyle.com*, http://www.tcboyle.com/page2.html?4 (accessed 22 April 2008).

2. Ibid.

3. Ibid.

4. Ibid.

5. Elizabeth Adams, "An Interview with T. Coraghessan Boyle," *Chicago Review* 37, no. 2–3 (1991): 59.

6. Judith Handschuh, "T. Coraghessan Boyle," *Bookreporter*, 1998–2000, http://www.bookreporter.com/authors/au-boyle-coraghessan.asp (accessed 5 June 2007).

7. Adams, "An Interview," 59.

8. Boyle, "This Monkey, My Back."

9. David L. Ulin, "The Science of Sex: T. C. Boyle on His *Inner Circle*, Alfred Kinsey and the Fine Line between Fact and Fiction," *TCBoyle.com*, 3–9 September 2004, http://www.tcboyle.com/author/laweekly.html (accessed 5 June 2007).

10. Patricia Lamberti, "Interview with T. C. Boyle," *Other Voices* 33 (Fall–Winter 2000), http://www.webdelsol.com/Other_Voices/BoyleInt.htm (accessed 5 June 2007).

11. T. C. Boyle, *Water Music* (Boston: Little, Brown, 1981), 3.

Chapter 2—T. C. Boyle's Short Fiction

1. T. C. Boyle, ed., *Doubletakes: Pairs of Contemporary Stories* (Belmont, Calif.: Heinle, 2003). References to this volume are hereafter cited parenthetically in the text.

2. Patricia Lamberti, "Interview with T. C. Boyle," *Other Voices* 33 (Fall–Winter 2000), http://www.webdelsol.com/Other_Voices/BoyleInt.htm (accessed 5 June 2007).

3. Charles Darwin, *The Origin of Species by Means of Natural Selection* and *The Descent of Man and Selection in Relation to Sex*,

Great Books of the Western World, ed. Robert Maynard Hutchins (Chicago: Encyclopedia Britannica, 1978), 253.

4. Nathan Leslie, "Interview with T. C. Boyle," *Pedestal Magazine,* http://www.thepedestalmagazine.com/secure/content/cb.asp?cbid=4690 (accessed 5 June 2007).

5. Denis Hennessey, "T. Coraghessan Boyle," in *American Short Story Writers since World War II: Second Series*, ed. Patrick Meanor and Gwen Crane, Dictionary of Literary Biography (Detroit: Bruccoli Clark Layman, 2000), 71.

6. The story "Descent of Man" appeared in Boyle's *Descent of Man: Stories* (Boston: Little, Brown / Atlantic Monthly, 1979); it was reprinted in *T. C. Boyle Stories: The Collected Stories of T. Coraghessan Boyle* (New York: Viking, 1998); quotation on page 97. Page citations, hereafter given parenthetically in the text, refer to the *T. C. Boyle Stories* version.

7. Hennessey, "T. Coraghessan Boyle," 72.

8. The stories "Greasy Lake" and "All Shook Up" appeared in Boyle's *Greasy Lake and Other Stories* (New York: Viking, 1985); they were reprinted in *T. C. Boyle Stories: The Collected Stories of T. Coraghessan Boyle* (New York: Viking, 1998). Page citations, hereafter given parenthetically in the text, refer to the *T. C. Boyle Stories* versions.

9. Michael Walker, "Boyle's 'Greasy Lake' and the Moral Failure of Postmodernism," *Studies in Short Fiction* 31, no. 2 (1994): 253.

10. The stories "If the River Was Whiskey" and "Sorry Fugu" appeared in Boyle's *If the River Was Whiskey: Stories* (New York: Viking, 1989); they were reprinted in *T. C. Boyle Stories: The Collected Stories of T. Coraghessan Boyle* (New York: Viking, 1998). Page citations, hereafter given parenthetically in the text, refer to the *T. C. Boyle Stories* versions.

11. Dan Pope, "A Different Kind of Post-Modernism," *Gettysburg Review* 3, no. 4 (1990): 661.

12. Ibid., 664.

13. Hennessey, "T. Coraghessan Boyle," 75.

14. The stories discussed in depth in this section, "Filthy with Things" and "Sitting on top of the World," appeared in Boyle's *Without a Hero: Stories* (New York: Viking, 1994); they were reprinted in *T. C. Boyle Stories: The Collected Stories of T. Coraghessan Boyle* (New York: Viking, 1998). Page citations, hereafter given parenthetically in the text, refer to the *T. C. Boyle Stories* versions.

15. "After the Plague" and "She Wasn't Soft" appeared in Boyle's *After the Plague and Other Stories* (New York: Viking, 2001); references to them are hereafter cited parenthetically in the text.

16. Lamberti, "Interview with T. C. Boyle."

17. "T. Coraghessan Boyle: Interview," *Failbetter,* Fall–Winter 2003, http://www.failbetter.com/12/BoyleInterview.htm (accessed 5 June 2007).

18. "The Kind Assassin" and "Up against the Wall" appeared in Boyle's *Tooth and Claw and Other Stories* (New York: Viking, 2005); references to them are hereafter cited parenthetically in the text.

19. Robert Birnbaum, "Personalities: Birnbaum v. T. C. Boyle," *Morning News: Black and White and Read All Over*, 10 January 2005, http://www.themorningnews.org/archives/personalities/birnbaum_v_tc_boyle.php (accessed 5 June 2007).

20. Tad Friend, "Rolling Boyle," *New York Times,* 9 December 1990, http://www.nytimes.com/books/98/02/08/home/boyle-rolling.html (accessed 22 April 2008).

Chapter 3—T. C. Boyle's Novels of the 1980s

1. Frederick R. Karl, "American Fictions: The Mega-Novel," *Scenewash,* 23 January 2004, http://www.scenewash.org/lobbies/artwatcher/ipings/literarychip/auspices/karl.html (accessed 23 April 2008).

2. Nathan Leslie, "Interview with T. C. Boyle," *Pedestal Magazine,* http://www.thepedestalmagazine.com/secure/content/cb.asp?cbid=4690 (accessed 5 June 2007).

3. See, for example, Shaun O'Connell, "A Crazed Humorist's Wild-and-Wooly Romp," *Boston Sun*, 14 February 1982, *TCBoyle .com,* http://www.tcboyle.com/page2.html?3 (accessed 4 June 2007).

4. Denis Hennessey, "T. Coraghessan Boyle," in *American Short Story Writers since World War II: Second Series*, ed. Patrick Meanor and Gwen Crane, Dictionary of Literary Biography (Detroit: Bruccoli Clark Layman, 2000), 71.

5. T. C. Boyle, *Water Music* (Boston: Little, Brown, 1981); quotations from this volume are hereafter cited parenthetically in the text.

6. Mary Heebner, "Interview with T. C. Boyle," *Mary Heebner* (official Web site), 2000, http://www.maryheebner.com/thework/ editorial/mungo_park/mungopark.html (accessed 5 June 2007).

7. Ibid.

8. See Mungo Park, *Travels in the Interior Districts of Africa*, ed. Kate Ferguson Marsters (Durham, N.C.: Duke University Press, 2000), 147–80.

9. Ibid., 162.

10. Justin D. Coffin, "20 Questions: T. Coraghessan Boyle," *Philadelphia Citypaper,* 26 February–5 March 1998, http://www .citypaper.net/articles/022698/20Q.Boyle.shtml (accessed 5 June 2007).

11. Paul Henry Lang, *George Frideric Handel* (New York: Norton, 1966), 133, 142.

12. Robert Birnbaum, "Personalities: Birnbaum v. T. C. Boyle," *Morning News: Black and White and Read All Over*, 10 January 2005, http://www.themorningnews.org/archives/personalities/ birnbaum_v_tc_boyle.php (accessed 5 June 2007).

13. Elizabeth Adams, "An Interview with T. Coraghessan Boyle," *Chicago Review* 37, no. 2–3 (1991): 58.

14. Jeff Simon, "Wild, Dark Novel in Grand Manner, a Bravura Performance," *Buffalo Evening News*, 14 February 1982, *TC Boyle.com,* http://www.tcboyle.com/page2.html?3 (accessed 4 June 2007).

15. T. C. Boyle, *Budding Prospects: A Pastoral* (New York: Viking, 1984); quotations from this volume are hereafter cited parenthetically in the text.

16. Bonnie Lyons, "T. Coraghessan Boyle." *American Novelists since World War II: Seventh Series*, ed. James R. Giles and Wanda H. Giles, Dictionary of Literary Biography (Detroit: Bruccoli Clark Layman, 2003), 75.

17. M. H. Abrams, *A Glossary of Literary Terms* (New York: Holt, Rinehart and Winston, 1981), 127.

18. Richard Eder, "Free Enterprise for Controlled Substance," Los Angeles Times Book Review, 6 May 1984, *TCBoyle.com*, http://www.tcboyle.com/page2.html?3 (accessed 4 June 2007).

19. Lyons, "T. Coraghessan Boyle," 75.

20. T. C. Boyle, *World's End* (New York: Viking, 1987); quotations from this volume are hereafter cited parenthetically in the text.

21. Adams, "An Interview," 58.

22. Coffin, "20 Questions."

23. C. P. Farley, "Tune In, Turn On, and Drop Out with T. C. Boyle," *Powells,* 26 March 2003, http://www.powells.com/authors/boyle.html (accessed 5 June 2007).

24. Friend, "Rolling Boyle."

25. John J. Curran, "Peekskill History," *City of Peekskill,* January 2002, http://www.ci.peekskill.ny.us/page.cfm?pageID=4 (accessed 9 June 2006).

26. Michael Kammen, "T. Coraghessan Boyle and *World's End*," in *Novel History: Historians and Novelists Confront America's Past (and Each Other)*, ed. Mark C. Carnes (New York: Simon & Schuster, 2001), 253.

27. Michiko Kakutani, review of *World's End,* by T. Coraghessan Boyle, *New York Times*, 23 September 1987. Available online at http://www.tcboyle.com/page2.html?3 (accessed 4 June 2007).

28. Kammen, "T. Coraghessan Boyle and *World's End*," 249.

29. T. C. Boyle, "History on Two Wheels," in *Novel History: Historians and Novelists Confront America's Past (and Each Other)*, ed. Mark C. Carnes (New York: Simon & Schuster, 2001), 260.

30. Theo D'haen, "The Return of History and the Minorization of New York: T. Coraghessan Boyle and Richard Russo," *Revue française d'études américaines* 17, no. 62 (1994): 398.

Chapter 4—T. C. Boyle's Novels of the 1990s

1. Robert Birnbaum, "T. C. Boyle: Author of *Drop City* Talks with Robert Birnbaum," *Identitytheory.com: A Literary Website, Sort of*, 19 March 2003, http://www.identitytheory.com/interviews/birnbaum94.html (accessed 5 June 2007).

2. Judith Handschuh, "T. Coraghessan Boyle," *Bookreporter*, 1998–2000, http://www.bookreporter.com/authors/au-boyle-coraghessan.asp (accessed 5 June 2007).

3. Bonnie Lyons, "T. Coraghessan Boyle." *American Novelists since World War II: Seventh Series*, ed. James R. Giles and Wanda H. Giles, Dictionary of Literary Biography (Detroit: Bruccoli Clark Layman, 2003), 77.

4. Lyons, "T. Coraghessan Boyle," 77.

5. T. C. Boyle, *East Is East* (New York: Viking, 1990); quotations from this volume are hereafter cited parenthetically in the text.

6. Elizabeth Adams, "An Interview with T. Coraghessan Boyle," *Chicago Review* 37, no. 2–3 (1991): 61–62.

7. 3. See Tsunetomo Yamamoto, *Bushido: The Way of the Samurai*, ed. Justine F. Stone, trans. Minoru Tanaka (Garden City Park, N.Y.: Square One, 2002).

8. Handschuh, "T. Coraghessan Boyle."

9. Heather J. Hicks, "On Whiteness in T. Coraghessan Boyle's *The Tortilla Curtain*," *Critique: Studies in Contemporary Fiction* 45, no. 1 (2003): 45.

10. Gail Godwin, "Samurai on the Run," *New York Times*, 9 September 1990. Available online at http://www.tcboyle.com/page2.html?3 (accessed 4 June 2007).

11. T. C. Boyle, *The Road to Wellville* (New York: Viking, 1993); quotations from this volume are hereafter cited parenthetically in the text.

12. Richard W. Schwarz, *John Harvey Kellogg, M.D.* (Nashville, Tenn.: Southern Publishing Association, 1970), 12–13, 240.

13. Schwarz, *John Harvey Kellogg, M.D.*

14. Ibid.

15. David Lipsky, "'Road to Wellville' Superb Work of Master Plotter," *Boston Globe*, 2 May 1993. Available online at http://www.tcboyle.com/page2.html?3 (accessed 4 June 2007).

16. Craig Seligman, "Survival of the Cruelest," *New Republic*, 4 October 1993, 44.

17. Mark Schechner, "Laughing from the Stomach Up," Buffalo News, 9 May 1993.

18. Quote from *TCBoyle.com*, Boyle's official Web site, http://www.tcboyle.com/page2.html?2 (accessed 9 July 2008). *The Tortilla Curtain* was published by Viking in 1995; quotations from the volume are hereafter cited parenthetically in the text.

19. Hicks, "On Whiteness," 46.

20. David Appell, "Earthquakes, Critics and the 600 Nitro: An Interview with T. Coraghessan Boyle," *Hayden's Ferry Review* 18 (Spring–Summer 1996), http://www.tcboyle.net/appell.html (accessed 1 October 2007).

21. Gregory Meyerson, "*Tortilla Curtain* and *The Ecology of Fear*," *Contracorriente: A Journal of Social History and Literature in Latin America* 2, no. 1 (2004): 70.

22. Geraldine Stoneham, "'It's a Free Country': Visions of Hybridity in the Metropolis," in *Comparing Postcolonial Literatures: Dislocations*, ed. Ashok Bery and Patricia Murray (New York: St. Martin's Press, 2000), 90.

23. Peter Freese, "T. Coraghessan Boyle's *The Tortilla Curtain*: A Case Study in the Genesis of Xenophobia," in *English Literatures in International Contexts*, ed. Heinz Antor and Klaus Stierstorfer (Heidelberg: Universitätsverlag C. Winter, 2000), 224.

24. Elisabeth Schäfer-Wünsche, "Borders and Catastrophes: T. C. Boyle's Californian Ecology," in *Space in America: Theory History Culture*, ed. Klaus Bensch and Kerstin Schmidt (Amsterdam: Rodopi, 2005), 405.

25. Roland Walter, "Notes on Border(land)s and Transculturation in the 'Damp and Hungry Interstices' of the Americas," in *How Far Is America from Here? Selected Proceedings of the First World Congress of the International American Studies Association, 22–24 May 2003*, ed. Theo D'haen, Djelal Kadir, and Lois Parkinson Zamora (Amsterdam: Rodopi, 2005), 143–44.

26. Appell, "Earthquakes, Critics and the 600 Nitro."

27. Heike Paul, "Old, New and 'Neo' Immigrant Fictions in American Literature: The Immigrant Presence in David Guterson's *Snow Falling on Cedars* and T. C. Boyle's *The Tortilla Curtain*," *Amerikastudien / American Studies* 46, no. 2 (2001): 263.

28. See Meyerson, "*Tortilla Curtain* and *The Ecology of Fear*," 87–88; and Hicks,"On Whiteness," 56–57.

29. Hicks, "On Whiteness," 57.

30. Ibid., 59.

31. Meyerson, "*Tortilla Curtain* and *The Ecology of Fear*," 79.

32. T. C. Boyle, *Riven Rock: A Novel* (New York: Viking, 1998); quotations from this volume are hereafter cited parenthetically in the text.

33. Laura Reynolds Adler, "Turning Fact into Fiction," *Book Page*, February 1998, http://www.bookpage.com/9802bp/tcboyle.html (accessed 5 June 2007).

34. Quote from *TCBoyle.com*, Boyle's official Web site, http://www.tcboyle.com/page2.html?2 (accessed 9 July 2008).

35. Adler, "Turning Fact into Fiction."

Chapter 5—T. C. Boyle's Novels of the 2000s

1. Robert Birnbaum, "T. C. Boyle: Author of *Drop City* Talks with Robert Birnbaum," *Identitytheory.com: A Literary Website, Sort of*, 19 March 2003, http://www.identitytheory.com/interviews/birnbaum94.html (accessed 5 June 2007).

2. T. C. Boyle, *A Friend of the Earth* (New York: Viking, 2000); quotations from the volume are hereafter cited parenthetically in the text.

3. Joe Knowles, "All This Useless Beauty," *In These Times*, 27 November 2000. Available online at http://www.tcboyle.com/page2 .html?3 (accessed 15 July 2008).

4. "T. Coraghessan Boyle: Interview," *Failbetter,* Fall–Winter 2003, http://www.failbetter.com/12/BoyleInterview.htm (accessed 5 June 2007).

5. Elisabeth Schäfer-Wünsche, "Borders and Catastrophes: T. C. Boyle's Californian Ecology," in *Space in America: Theory History Culture*, ed. Klaus Bensch and Kerstin Schmidt (Amsterdam: Rodopi, 2005), 414.

6. Gregory Daurer, "T. Coraghessan Boyle," *Salon,* 11 December 2000, http://archive.salon.com/people/conv/2000/12/11/boyle/ (accessed 5 June 2007).

7. Alan Gottlieb, "Unedited Transcript of Interview with T. Coraghessan Boyle," *Tcboyle.net,* 22 October 2000, http://www.tcboyle .net/gottlieb.html (accessed 5 June 2007).

8. Birnbaum, "T. C. Boyle: Author."

9. T. C. Boyle, *Drop City: A Novel* (New York: Viking, 2003); quotations from the volume are hereafter cited parenthetically in the text.

10. C. P. Farley, "Tune In, Turn On, and Drop Out with T. C. Boyle," *Powells,* 26 March 2003, http://www.powells.com/authors/ boyle.html (accessed 5 June 2007).

11. Dwight Garner, "'Drop City': How Flower Power Went to Seed," *New York Times Book Review*, 23 February 2003. Available online at http://www.tcboyle.com/page2.html?3 (accessed 4 June 2007).

12. T. C. Boyle, *The Inner Circle: A Novel* (New York: Viking, 2004); quotations from the volume are hereafter cited parenthetically in the text.

13. Sigmund Freud, *Civilization and Its Discontents*, trans. and ed. James Strachey (New York: Norton, 1989), 95.

14. Ibid.

15. T. C. Boyle, *Talk Talk* (New York: Viking, 2006); quotations from the volume are hereafter cited parenthetically in the text.

16. Paul Gleason, "Historical Responsibility and Postmodern Detective Fiction in Haruki Murakami's *The Wind-Up Bird Chronicle* and Kazuo Ishiguro's *When We Were Orphans*" (paper presented at the 2005 Midwest Modern Language Association Conference, Milwaukee, Wis., November 2005).

17. Michiko Kakutani, "A Stolen Identity in 'Talk Talk' by T. C. Boyle," *New York Times*, 4 July 2006, http://www.nytimes.com/2006/07/04/books/04kaku.html?ex=1181102400&en=49f0624536093157&ei=5070 (accessed 4 June 2007).

Bibliography

Primary Bibliography

My references to the stories originally published in *Descent of Man, Greasy Lake, If the River Was Whiskey*, and *Without a Hero* are to *T. C. Boyle Stories*, which collects all the stories published in these four books and adds seven previously unpublished tales. *T. C. Boyle Stories* is the standard edition of the stories Boyle published before *After the Plague*.

Books by T. C. Boyle

After the Plague and Other Stories. New York: Viking, 2001; London: Bloomsbury, 2001.

Budding Prospects: A Pastoral. New York: Viking, 1984; London: Gollancz, 1984.

The Collected Stories of T. Coraghessan Boyle. New York: Granta, 1993; London: Granta, 1993.

Descent of Man: Stories. Boston: Little, Brown / Atlantic Monthly, 1979; London: Gollancz, 1979.

Doubletakes: Pairs of Contemporary Stories. Edited by T. C. Boyle. Belmont, Calif.: Heinle, 2003.

Drop City: A Novel. New York: Viking, 2003; London: Bloomsbury, 2003.

East Is East. New York: Viking, 1990; London: Cape, 1991.

A Friend of the Earth. New York: Viking, 2000; London: Bloomsbury, 2000.

Greasy Lake and Other Stories. New York: Viking, 1985.

The Human Fly and Other Stories. New York: Viking, 2005.

If the River Was Whiskey: Stories. New York: Viking, 1989.

The Inner Circle: A Novel. New York: Viking, 2004; London: Bloomsbury, 2004.

Riven Rock: A Novel. New York: Viking, 1998; London: Bloomsbury, 1998.

The Road to Wellville. New York: Viking, 1993; London: Granta, 1993.

T. C. Boyle Stories: The Collected Stories of T. Coraghessan Boyle. New York: Viking, 1998.

Talk Talk. New York: Viking, 2006; London: Bloomsbury, 2006.

Tooth and Claw and Other Stories. New York: Viking, 2005; London: Bloomsbury, 2005.

The Tortilla Curtain. New York: Viking, 1995; London: Bloomsbury, 1995.

Water Music. Boston: Little, Brown, 1981; London: Gollancz, 1982.

Without a Hero: Stories. New York: Viking, 1994; London: Granta, 1994.

The Women: A Novel. New York: Viking, forthcoming, 2009.

World's End. New York: Viking, 1987; London: Macmillan, 1988.

Selected Uncollected Writings of T. C. Boyle

"Balto." *Paris Review* 179 (Winter 2006): 51–69.

"A Better Class of Fools." *New York Times Book Review*, 7 June 1987, 9.

"Charlie Ossining Goes Downtown, Thanks to Alan Parker." *Zoetrope All-Stories* 3 (Spring 1999), http://www.all-story.com/issues.cgi?action+show–story&story_id=35 (accessed 25 July 2008).

"A Christmas Story: Three Quarters of the Way to Hell." *Playboy*, December 2005, 72–75.

"Fondue." *Antioch Review* 59 (Spring 2001): 492–99.

"Full Boyle." Originally written for Amazon.com; now available online at http://www.englisch.schule.de/boyle/boyleaut.htm#Boyle (accessed 22 April 2008).

"The Great Divide." *New York Times Book Review*, 18 May 1997, 9.

"Guppies and the Apocalypse: On the Subject of Children." *Tcboyle.net*. 1997. http://www.tcboyle.net/guppies.html (accessed 22 April 2008).

"Hands On." *Kenyon Review* 29 (Summer 2007): 29–37.

"History on Two Wheels." In *Novel History: Historians and Novelists Confront America's Past (and Each Other)*, edited by Mark C. Carnes, 259–61. New York: Simon & Schuster, 2001.

"If I Were President." *George* 3 (February 1998): 120.

"In Search of the Striped Bass." *Life*, September 1992. Available online at http://www.tcboyle.net/bass.html (accessed 15 July 2008).

"Into the Heart of Borneo." *California* 12 (December 1987): 33.

"Into the Heart of Old Albany." *New York Times Book Review*, 22 May 1988, 1.

"La Conchita." *New Yorker,* 12 December 2005, 94–101.

"My Suburb: Santa Barbara, Calif." *New York Times Magazine*, 9 April 2000, 55.

"Nighttime in the Pool." *New Yorker*, 14 June 2004, 108–9.

"Politics and the Novel: A Symposium." *Los Angeles Times Book Review*, 13 August 2000. Available online at http://www.tcboyle.net/politics%26.html (accessed 15 July 2008).

"Question 62." *Harper's Magazine,* March 2006, 68–76.

"T. Rex, Lies, and Videotape: Is Virtual Reality the New Backyard?" *Forbes*, 2 October 2000. http://www.forbes.com/asap/2000/1002/066_print.html (accessed 22 April 2008).

"That Was the Century That Was." *Gentlemen's Quarterly,* December 1999, 183–90.

"This Monkey, My Back." *TCBoyle.com*. T. C. Boyle. http://www.tcboyle.com/page2.html?4 (accessed 22 April 2008).

"Three Minutes or Less." *Paris Review* 153 (Winter 1999–2000): 130–58. Boyle's contribution, "Heroes," is found on pages 137–38.

"To Pump or Not to Pump." *New York Times*, 30 April 2006. http://www.nytimes.com/2006/04/30/opinion/30boyle.html (accessed 30 July 2008).

"Top of the Food Chain." *Harper's Magazine,* April 1993, 72–75.

"The Unlucky Mother of Aquiles Maldonado." *Playboy,* September 2006, 74–77.

"A Voice Griping in the Wilderness." *New York Times Book Review*, 10 February 2002, 8.

"Waiting for the Apocalypse." *New York Times,* 29 October 2003, 25.

"What Is This Bee? Reading Lessons." *L.A. Weekly,* 26 February–4 March 1999. Available online at http://www.mondowendell.com/boyle.htm (accessed 30 July 2008).

"Who Is the Truest Parent?" *New York Times Book Review*, 7 January 1990. http://www.nytimes.com/books/98/06/28/specials/beattie-will.html (accessed 15 July 2008).

"Wild Child." *McSweeney's* 19 (10 April 2006).

Secondary Bibliography

Adams, Elizabeth. "An Interview with T. Coraghessan Boyle." *Chicago Review* 37, no. 2–3 (1991): 51–63.

Adler, Laura Reynolds. "Turning Fact into Fiction." *Book Page*, February 1998. http://www.bookpage.com/9802bp/tcboyle.html (accessed 5 June 2007).

Appell, David. "Earthquakes, Critics and the 600 Nitro: An Interview with T. Coraghessan Boyle." *Hayden's Ferry Review* 18 (Spring–Summer 1996). http://www.tcboyle.net/appell.html (accessed 1 October 2007).

Birnbaum, Robert. "Personalities: Birnbaum v. T. C. Boyle." *Morning News: Black and White and Read All Over*, 10 January 2005. http://www.themorningnews.org/archives/personalities/birnbaum_v_tc_boyle.php (accessed 5 June 2007).

———. "T. C. Boyle: Author of *Drop City* Talks with Robert Birnbaum." *Identitytheory.com: A Literary Website, Sort of,* 19 March 2003. http://www.identitytheory.com/interviews/birnbaum94.html (accessed 5 June 2007).

Brussin, Alana. "Finishing What You've Started: An Interview with T. Coraghessan Boyle." *Hayden's Ferry Review* 31 (Fall 2002–Winter 2003): 135–47.

Cheng, Terrence. "Interview with T. Coraghessan Boyle." *Crazyhorse* 51 (Winter 1996): 84–96.

Coffin, Justin D. "20 Questions: T. Coraghessan Boyle." *Philadelphia Citypaper,* 26 February–5 March 1998. http://www.citypaper.net/articles/022698/20Q.Boyle.shtml (accessed 5 June 2007).

Cotes, Peter. "Eastenders Go West: English Sparrows, Immigrants, and the Nature of Fear." *Journal of American Studies* 39 (December 2005): 431–62.

Dalrymple, Terrence A. "T. C. Boyle as a Tragedian, Robert Johnson as Tragic Hero: An Analysis of Boyle's Story 'Stones in My Passway, Hellhound on My Trail.'" *Short Story* 8 (Spring 2000): 69–77.

Daurer, Gregory. "T. Coraghessan Boyle." *Salon,* 11 December 2000. http://archive.salon.com/people/conv/2000/12/11/boyle/ (accessed 5 June 2007).

Dewey, Joseph. *Novels from Reagan's America: A New Realism.* Gainesville: University of Florida Press, 1999.

D'haen, Theo. "The Return of History and the Minorization of New York: T. Coraghessan Boyle and Richard Russo." *Revue française d'études américaines* 17, no. 62 (1994): 393–403.

Douglas, Christopher. *Reciting America: Culture and Cliché in Contemporary U.S. Fiction.* Urbana: University of Illinois Press, 2001.
———. "Tracking 'The Wild Man of the Green Swamp': Orientalism, Clichés, and the Preoccupation of Language." *English Studies in Canada* 23 (September 1997): 331–55.

Failbetter. "T. Coraghessan Boyle: Interview." *Failbetter,* Fall–Winter 2003. http://www.failbetter.com/12/BoyleInterview.htm (accessed 5 June 2007).

Farley, C. P. "Tune In, Turn On, and Drop Out with T. C. Boyle." *Powells,* 26 March 2003. http://www.powells.com/authors/boyle.html (accessed 5 June 2007).

Freese, Peter. "T. Coraghessan Boyle's *The Tortilla Curtain*: A Case Study in the Genesis of Xenophobia." In *English Literatures in International Contexts*, edited by Heinz Antor and Klaus Stierstorfer, 221–43. Heidelberg: Universitätsverlag C. Winter, 2000.

Friend, Tad. "Rolling Boyle." *New York Times,* 9 December 1990. http://www.nytimes.com/books/98/02/08/home/boyle-rolling .html (accessed 22 April 2008).

Goldblatt, Patricia. "School Is Still the Place: Stories of Immigration and Education." *MultiCultural Review* 13, no. 1 (2004): 49–54.

Gottlieb, Alan. "Unedited Transcript of Interview with T. Coraghessan Boyle." *Tcboyle.net,* 22 October 2000. http://www.tcboyle .net/gottlieb.html (accessed 5 June 2007).

Gray, Lynn. "An Interview with T. Coraghessan Boyle." *Short Story Review* 5 (Spring 1988): 2–3, 6.

Handschuh, Judith. "T. Coraghessan Boyle." *Bookreporter,* 1998–2000. http://www.bookreporter.com/authors/au-boyle -coraghessan.asp (accessed 5 June 2007).

Heebner, Mary. "Interview with T. C. Boyle." *Mary Heebner* (official Web site), 2000. http://www.maryheebner.com/thework/ editorial/mungo_park/mungopark.html (accessed 5 June 2007).

Hennessey, Denis. "T. Coraghessan Boyle." In *American Short Story Writers since World War II: Second Series*, edited by Patrick Meanor and Gwen Crane, 70–77. Dictionary of Literary Biography. Detroit: Bruccoli Clark Layman, 2000.

Hicks, Heather J. "On Whiteness in T. Coraghessan Boyle's *The Tortilla Curtain.*" *Critique: Studies in Contemporary Fiction* 45 (Fall 2003): 43–64.

Hume, Kathryn. *American Dream, American Nightmare: Fiction since 1960*. Urbana: University of Illinois Press, 2000.

Kammen, Michael. "T. Coraghessan Boyle and *World's End.*" In *Novel History: Historians and Novelists Confront America's Past (and Each Other)*, edited by Mark C. Carnes, 245–58. New York: Simon & Schuster, 2001.

Lamberti, Patricia. "Interview with T. C. Boyle." *Other Voices* 33 (Fall–Winter 2000). http://www.webdelsol.com/Other_Voices/ BoyleInt.htm (accessed 5 June 2007).

Law, Danielle. "Caught in the Current: Plotting History in *Water Music.*" *In-Between: Essays and Studies in Literary Criticism* 5 (March 1995): 41–50.

Leslie, Nathan. "Interview with T. C. Boyle." *Pedestal Magazine.* http://www.thepedestalmagazine.com/secure/content/cb.asp?cbid =4690 (accessed 5 June 2007).

Lyons, Bonnie. "Entertainments and Provocations." *Passion and Craft: Conversations with Notable Writers,* edited by Bonnie Lyons and Bill Oliver, 42–59. Urbana: University of Illinois Press, 1998.

———. "T. Coraghessan Boyle." In *American Novelists since World War II: Seventh Series,* edited by James R. Giles and Wanda H. Giles, 73–80. Dictionary of Literary Biography. Detroit: Bruccoli Clark Layman, 2003.

Meyerson, Gregory. "*Tortilla Curtain* and *The Ecology of Fear.*" *Contracorriente: A Journal of Social History and Literature in Latin America* 2, no. 1 (2004): 67–91.

Paul, Heike. "Old, New and 'Neo' Immigrant Fictions in American Literature: The Immigrant Presence in David Guterson's *Snow Falling on Cedars* and T. C. Boyle's *The Tortilla Curtain.*" *Amerikastudien/American Studies* 46, no. 2 (2001): 249–65.

Pope, Dan. "A Different Kind of Post-Modernism." *Gettysburg Review* 3, no. 4 (1990): 65–69.

Raabe, David M. "Boyle's 'Descent of Man.'" *Explicator* 58 (Summer 2000): 223–26.

Salvini, Laura. "'Our Wall': Octavia E. Butler's *Parable of the Sower* and T. Coraghessan Boyle's *The Tortilla Curtain.*" In *America Today: Highways and Labyrinths: Proceedings of the XV Biennial Conference Siracusa, November 4–7, 1999,* edited by Gigliola Nocera, 264–72. Siracusa: Grafià Editrice, 2003.

Schäfer-Wünsche, Elisabeth. "Borders and Catastrophes: T. C. Boyle's Californian Ecology." In *Space in America: Theory History Culture,* edited by Klaus Bensch and Kerstin Schmidt, 401–17. Amsterdam: Rodopi, 2005.

Schenker, Daniel. "A Samurai in the South: Cross-Cultural Disaster in T. Coraghessan Boyle's *East Is East.*" *Southern Quarterly: A Journal of the Arts in the South* 34 (Fall 1995): 70–80.

Shelffo, Andrew. "'Wait 'til Next Year': The Red Sox, T. Coraghessan Boyle, and a Year in New England." *Aethelon: The Journal of Sport Literature* 21 (Spring 2004): 15–23.

Spencer, Nicholas. "Inhuman(e) Subjects: Postmodern Theory and Contemporary Animal Liberation." In *From Virgin Land to Disney World: Nature and Its Discontents in the USA of Yesterday and Today,* edited by Bernd Herzogenrath, 187–208. Amsterdam: Rodopi, 2001.

Stoneham, Geraldine. "'It's a Free Country': Visions of Hybridity in the Metropolis." In *Comparing Postcolonial Literatures: Dislocations,* edited by Ashok Bery and Patricia Murray, 81–92. New York: St. Martin's Press, 2000.

Ulin, David L. "The Science of Sex: T. C. Boyle on His *Inner Circle,* Alfred Kinsey and the Fine Line between Fact and Fiction." *TCBoyle.com.* T. C. Boyle. 3–9 September 2004. http://www.tcboyle.com/author/laweekly.html (accessed 5 June 2007).

Vaid, Krishna Baldev. "Franz Kafka Writes to T. Coraghessan Boyle." *Michigan Quarterly Review* 35 (Summer 1996): 53–57.

Walker, Michael. "Boyle's 'Greasy Lake' and the Moral Failure of Postmodernism." *Studies in Short Fiction* 31, no. 2 (1994): 247–55.

Walter, Roland. "Notes on Border(land)s and Transculturation in the 'Damp and Hungry Interstices' of the Americas." In *How Far Is America from Here? Selected Proceedings of the First World Congress of the International American Studies Association, 22–24 May 2003,* edited by Theo D'haen, Djelal Kadir, and Lois Parkinson Zamora, 143–57. Amsterdam: Rodopi, 2005.

Wild, Peter. "Peter Wild Interviews T. C. Boyle." *3:AM Magazine,* June 2003. http://www.3ammagazine.com/litarchives/2003/jun/interview_tc_boyle.html (accessed 5 June 2007).

Index

References are to the historical personages unless otherwise noted. References to literary works are works by T. C. Boyle unless otherwise noted.